Radio Mastery for VFR Pilots Workbook

Brain Training for VFR Radio Procedures

By

Jeff Kanarish

Printed in the United States of America

First Printing, 2013

ISBN 978-0615824239

Personal Media Works, LLC
P.O. Box 190846
Atlanta, GA 30119

The individuals and aircraft identities used in this workbook are fictitious. Any resemblance to actual people and aircraft is purely coincidental. The names of most air traffic control agencies used in this book are real, except where noted. All air traffic control scenarios described in this book, though inspired by the author's real-world experience, are works of fiction.

All charts and diagrams in this workbook are for instructional purposes only. They are not intended for use in actual navigation.

Acknowledgments

The workbook you are about to enjoy was made possible with the generous help of the following pilots:

Rob Cavanaugh, Gary Harvancik, John Herman, Greg Hughes, Alan Lasneski , Brian Mahan, Marshall Mann, Thor Mikesell, Dave Pompea, Mark Potter, and Nathan Rose. Gentlemen, thank you for your time and effort. Your careful edits and insights were invaluable.

Thank you to my good friend Robin Maiden for suggesting the idea behind this workbook and for inspiring me to see it through to completion.

To you dear reader, thank you for spending time with me in my written work and at our website. Your questions, comments and enthusiastic support drive me to push the envelope.

Finally, to my wife Dawn, thank you for your advice, your meticulous attention to detail, and your unconditional support and love. Onward we go, hand in hand. Love you, Hon.

A workbook for radio work?

How is reading and writing going to help you communicate on the radio? Isn't radio work all about speaking and listening? Not really.

In addition to speaking and listening, there is a whole lot of brainwork going on to make a decent radio transmission. If you read my book *Radio Mastery for VFR Pilots*, you'll recognize this checklist for making radio transmissions:

1. Listen.

2. Engage brain.

3. Speak.

Using this workbook, I'll help you primarily with Item 2 in that checklist. I'm going to train your brain to file, organize, retrieve, and deliver the right response on the radio at the right time. Here is how I'm going to do that for you.

First, I'm going to help you visualize different flying scenarios where timely radio work is essential. Sure, you could bypass visualizing your flying environment and try to force your brain to store radio calls by rote memorization. Rote memorization rarely produces long-lasting results. Radio calls crammed into your memory have about the same half-life as facts learned by cramming for a final exam in school.

What do you remember from Psychology 101? Next to nothing, I suspect. I suspect that because I remember next to nothing from Psychology 101, even though my school transcript shows I got an A in the class. I got that A by cramming for the mid-term and final exams. Cramming for the exam produced excellent short-term results. It did nothing for long-term memory. Luckily, there is an alternative to cramming that produces long-term retention of learned information.

By plugging radio calls into real-life scenarios, you can build strong associations between mental imagery and the words you would use in those scenarios. Let's be clear. I'm not talking only about simply reading stories, I'm talking about immersing yourself in a situation in which you can visualize and hear what is going on. It may sound off-the-wall now, but a few short minutes from now, when you actually try it, this method will make sense.

Second, you are going to look at radio work from both ends of the communication link. Not only am I going to ask you to think as a pilot, I'm also going to ask you to think as though you are an air traffic controller.

What?! I know, you didn't sign up to be an air traffic controller. Nobody panic.

In every section of this workbook, you will be taking off your pilot's cap and putting on an air traffic controller's cap for a few minutes. By looking at radio communication through the eyes of an air traffic controller, you will get a firmer grip on what to expect from ATC in any flying situation. This method is one of the secret ingredients in a process that will make you a more confident communicator on the aircraft radio.

But wait, there's more! As a special bonus, just for picking up this workbook, I'm going to throw in, at no additional cost to you, training in checklist item 3: Speak! That's right. Act now and I'll throw in speaking exercises as a special thank you, just for picking up this workbook.

Before we get to it, please consider picking up a copy of *Radio Mastery for VFR Pilots*. This workbook steps through exercises that follow the same order of material presented in *Radio Mastery for VFR Pilots*. Although you could run through this workbook without reading *Radio Mastery for VFR Pilots*, using both books will add a depth of knowledge that would be difficult to find anywhere else.

Enough preamble. Let's set you up for success on the aircraft radio.

Making the Workbook Work for You

This is a workbook of questions and answers. I ask the question. You write the answer. Then I give you the ideal answer to compare with your answer. This comes as no great surprise, right?

Here is where this workbook differs from others you may have used. Most workbooks have an answer key at the end of each chapter, or worse, in the last section of the workbook. I find it difficult, and a bit frustrating to flip back and forth between questions in one section and the answer key in another section, don't you?

In this workbook, each answer is directly below the question. Of course, you will want to avoid seeing the answer before you have made your attempt at answering the question on your own. Here's how.

Answer Cover

The next 2 pages in this workbook are answer key covers. (I included 2 pages in case one becomes lost or unusable.) I recommend using a scissors or a razor knife to cut each cover from the workbook, following the cutting guideline on each page. If you make a mistake cutting the covers from the workbook, or if you would prefer not to use the included covers, any opaque material such as cardboard, may be substituted.

Using the Cover

Place the answer cover on the workbook page you will be using. Slide the cover down the page, until you see this line:

↓↓**ANSWER**↓↓

Stop! Go no further. The answer to the question is just below that line. (Note: In some cases, the line may be on the bottom of the page. In that case, the answer is at the top of the following page.)

Answer the question. When you are ready to see the correct answer, slide the cover down just enough to reveal the answer. Then, slide the cover further down the page to reveal the next exercise and the next answer line. Repeat the process for each new exercise.

Visualization and Verbalization

Many exercises will ask you to visualize the scenario presented to you in the exercise. Visualization is critical to training your brain to respond correctly in the future when you encounter a similar situation in your airplane. Please follow the visualization directions when they are presented. You will be rewarded with much better training results if you do.

You will also see " 🎧 Now, say it out loud" in the answer area for many exercises. The radio headset and written prompt reminds you to speak the ideal radio transmission out loud. If you feel embarrassed to speak radio transmissions out loud because others might hear you, find a place where you can complete this vital part of the learning process in private. Verbalizing radio transmissions out loud is absolutely critical to learning and memory.

You may also work through these exercises with a training partner. One partner plays ATC and says the clearance described in the workbook. The other partner plays the pilot and responds to the clearance. The pilot's response may then be checked against the correct response in the workbook. Give it a try!

Ground Rules and Air Rules

We pilots are used to operating with a framework of rules, also known as the Consolidated Federal Regulations, Part 91. I'm going to give you a framework of rules for operating inside this workbook. Unlike the federal regs, the rules for this workbook are short, simple, and easy to follow. Also unlike the federal regs, no one is going to haul you in front of a review panel and tell you to turn in your license if you decide to blow off the rules. These rules are offered to make the workbook more effective. Use or modify them at your discretion.

Jeff's Rules of Workbook Use

1. Begin at the beginning. Each exercise and section builds upon the previous exercise and section.

2. Work through the exercises in order, but . . .

3. Once you have a firm grip on how to make a particular radio call, don't feel obligated to finish every exercise in a section. Take what you need and move on.

4. You are welcome to skip whole sections of material you already know. Use caution when skipping sections, however. There are some tips and tricks in each section you might not have heard before.

5. Many exercises ask you to write out the radio transmission you would make for the given situation. I have included the ideal radio transmission in the answer key below each exercise. Although there are acceptable variations on some radio calls, the ideal answers follow standard phraseology described in the Aeronautical Information Manual (AIM).

6. Some exercises ask you about general knowledge on a topic. Don't write an essay. One-sentence or 2-sentence answers are good enough.

7. When answering general knowledge questions, your answer does not have to match my answer word for word. Consider your answer correct when it provides the essential facts included in my answer.

8. In the answers I provide for many radio transmission exercises, I include notes or explanations that support the answer. The answer you write does not have to include my notes or explanations to be correct. Where applicable I cite the source for the answer in the AIM, in my book *Radio Mastery for VFR Pilots*, or in both. A free online version of the AIM, is available at: www.faa.gov/air_traffic/publications/ATpubs/AIM/aim.pdf.

9. If you have any questions about any of the material or exercises, feel free to write to me at jeff@ATCcommunication.com.

10. Have fun!

✂ Cut Here

Numbers and Letters

The pronunciation of numbers is abused by pilots the world over. That slack approach to speaking numbers amazes me. It does not take much imagination to consider all the trouble you could get into in your airplane when either you or an air traffic controller misunderstands a number related to your flight path. For example, if a controller misunderstands your readback of an assigned altitude, you have no backup from ATC against busting through an assigned altitude, or descending into a mountainside. Misunderstanding your readback of an assigned heading may result in you flying into restricted airspace. The list goes on.

Saying numbers according to the way the Aeronautical Information Manual (AIM 4-2-8) says you should say them is critical. It is critical to hanging on to your pilot's license, to your passengers' safety, and to your life.

By the way, the AIM says you should pronounce 3, 5, and 9 as "tree", "fife", and "niner" respectively. Niner gets good use on the radio by pilots and air traffic controllers, probably because it gets a lot of play by Hollywood actors in classic movies about flying. Not so much for tree and fife.

Most pilots and the majority of air traffic controllers do not use the official pronunciations for 3 and 5 and yet, the ATC system continues to operate safely. Although I hesitate to say this, especially after I just told you to say numbers the way the AIM says you should say them, I cannot fault you if you say "three" and "five" when speaking on your aircraft radio. Let's practice by flipping to the next page and saying some numbers.

Altitudes

Write how you would speak the following numbers. Be sure to write out the numbers in the blank area to the right of the instrument. Example: If the altimeter indicates 2,000, write: Two thousand.

1.

SEVEN HUNDRED

↓↓**ANSWER**↓↓

Seven hundred.

Now, say it out loud:

2.

THOUSAND
TWO THREE HUNDRED

↓↓**ANSWER**↓↓

Two thousand tree hundred.

Now, say it out loud:

3.

One Two Thousand Tree Hundred (handwritten)

↓↓**ANSWER**↓↓

One two thousand tree hundred.

🎧 Now, say it out loud:

4.

One Thousand Fits Hundred (handwritten)

↓↓**ANSWER**↓↓

One thousand fife hundred.

🎧 Now, say it out loud:

5.

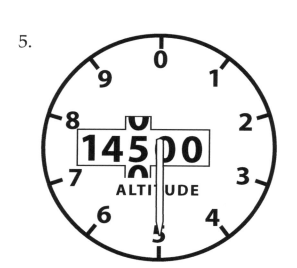

ONE FOUR THOUSAND
FIFE HUNDRD

↓↓**ANSWER**↓↓

One four thousand fife hundred.

 Now, say it out loud:

6.

SIXTHOUSAND
ONE HUNDRD

↓↓**ANSWER**↓↓

Six thousand one hundred.

Now, say it out loud:

7.

ONE
THOUSAND

↓↓**ANSWER**↓↓

One thousand.

🎧 Now, say it out loud:

Vertical Speeds

Write how you would speak the following vertical speeds. Be sure to write out "climbing" or descending" plus the numbers and "feet per minute." For example, with an indication of 2,000 rate of climb, write: Climbing two thousand feet per minute. (Note: Due to the non-precision marking on some vertical speed indicators, your answer may be slightly different than what is shown in the answer key. If your answer differs by + or – 200 feet per minute from the answer key, that is acceptable.) Let's practice using numbers in vertical speeds by flipping to the next page.

1.

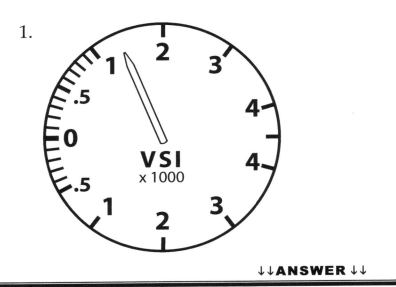

↓↓**ANSWER**↓↓

Climbing one thousand tree hundred feet per minute.

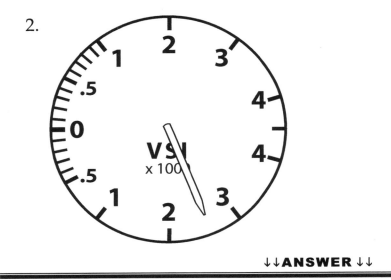 Now, say it out loud:

2.

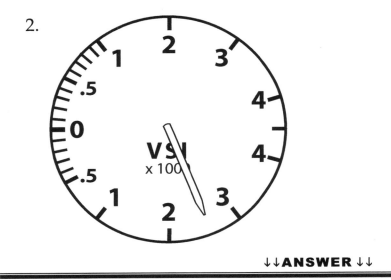

↓↓**ANSWER**↓↓

Descending two thousand six hundred feet per minute.

Now, say it out loud:

3.

↓↓**ANSWER**↓↓

Climbing fife hundred feet per minute.

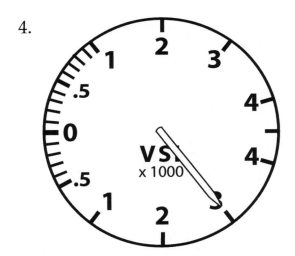 Now, say it out loud:

4.

↓↓**ANSWER**↓↓

Descending tree thousand feet per minute.

Now, say it out loud:

Headings

Write how you would speak the following headings. Be sure to spell out the numbers. For example: if the heading indicator shows 090, write: Heading zero niner zero.

1.

Heading Two Four Zer (handwritten)

↓↓**ANSWER**↓↓

Heading two four zero.

◗ Now, say it out loud:

2.

Heading Tree Fife Fife (handwritten)

↓↓**ANSWER**↓↓

Heading tree fife fife.

◗ Now, say it out loud:

3.

*Heading
Tree Six Zero*

↓↓**ANSWER**↓↓

Heading tree six zero.

 Now, say it out loud:

4.

*Heading
One Seven Zero*

↓↓**ANSWER**↓↓

Heading one seven zero.

 Now, say it out loud:

Airspeed

Write how you would speak the following airspeeds. Be sure to write out the numbers, plus "knots." For example, if the airspeed indicator shows 120, write: One two zero knots.

1.

ONE TREE ZERO KNOTS

↓↓**ANSWER** ↓↓

One tree zero knots.

Now, say it out loud:

2.

ONE ONE ZERO KNOTS

↓↓**ANSWER** ↓↓

One one zero knots.

Now, say it out loud:

3.

NINER ZERO KNOTS

↓↓**ANSWER**↓↓

Niner zero knots.

Now, say it out loud:

4.

ONE ONE FIFE KNOTS

↓↓**ANSWER**↓↓

One one fife knots.

Now, say it out loud:

Letters

Write out the phonetic spelling for the underlined letters in the following descriptions. For example, if the underlined letter is X, write Xray. If multiple letters are underlined, write out the phonetic spelling for each letter in the combination. You do not have to write out the words preceding or following the underlined letters. You will find a listing of the phonetic alphabet in AIM Table 4-2-2.

1. Taxiway <u>P</u>

2. The Northbrook VORTAC (<u>OBK</u>)

3. Airway <u>V</u>-171

4. The <u>MUFTI</u> intersection

5. The Scholes International Airport (<u>GLS</u>)

6. The Carolina Beach NDB (<u>CLB</u>)

7. The Dixon Airport (<u>DWX</u>)

8. The Hanksville VORTAC (<u>HVE</u>)

9. Taxiway <u>Z</u>

10. The <u>NOJAY</u> intersection

11. The Dupont VORTAC (<u>DQO</u>)

12. Taxiway <u>R</u>

↓↓ANSWER↓↓

1. Papa

2. Oscar Bravo Kilo

3. Victor

4. Mike Uniform Foxtrot Tango India

5. Golf Lima Sierra

6. Charlie Lima Bravo

7. Delta Whiskey Xray

8. Hotel Victor Echo

9. Zulu

10. November Oscar Juliett Alpha Yankee

11. Delta Quebec Oscar

12. Romeo

Think Like a Controller—Numbers and Letters Readback/Hearback

Below you will find ATC clearances followed by a pilot's response. Imagine that you are an air traffic controller, responsible for listening to the readback of clearances made by pilots. Write Correct or Incorrect in the blank for each pilot response. (Note: For this exercise, call signs are intentionally omitted.)

1.   "Turn right heading one four zero. Reduce speed to one four zero."

_____ "Right heading one four zero, speed one four zero."

↓↓ANSWER↓↓

Correct.

2.   "Descend and maintain fife thousand."

_____ "Fife thousand."

↓↓ANSWER↓↓

Acceptable, but a better readback is: "Descend and maintain fife thousand."

3.   "Turn left heading two seven zero, maintain two one zero knots."

_____ "Left heading two seven zero, two-ten on the speed."

↓↓ANSWER↓↓

Incorrect. Correct readback: "Left heading two seven zero. Two one zero knots."

4. "Climb and maintain four thousand."

_____ "On up to four."

↓↓**ANSWER**↓↓

Incorrect. Correct readback: "Climb and maintain four thousand."

5. "Turn left two zero degrees."

_____ "Left twenty degrees."

↓↓**ANSWER**↓↓

Incorrect. Correct readback: "Left two zero degrees."

6. "Maintain two zero zero knots."

_____ "Maintain two zero zero."

↓↓**ANSWER**↓↓

Incorrect. Correct readback: "Two zero zero knots."

7. "Fly direct Muscle Shoals. Maintain fife thousand."

_____ "Direct Muscle Shoals. Maintain fife thousand."

↓↓**ANSWER**↓↓

Correct.

8.   "Say your heading."

_____ "Heading is one thirty."

↓↓ANSWER↓↓

Incorrect. Correct reply: "Heading is one tree zero."

9.   "Maintain at least one thousand fife hundred feet per minute in your rate of descent."

_____ "We'll maintain at least one thousand fife hundred feet per minute in our descent."

↓↓ANSWER↓↓

Correct.

10.   "Climb and maintain one tree thousand."

_____ "Climb and maintain thirteen thousand."

↓↓ANSWER↓↓

Incorrect. Correct readback: "Climb and maintain one tree thousand."

11.   "Say your altitude passing."

_____ "Passing fife thousand eight hundred."

↓↓ANSWER↓↓

Correct.

12. "Verify the intersection the previous controller cleared you to." (Note: You were cleared direct YETTI.)

_____ "We were cleared direct Yankee Echo Tango Tango India."

Correct.

Note: You are not required to spell intersections when speaking to ATC. Spelling is only used as needed to aid in understanding the name. In this example, it would be acceptable to say the name of the intersection and not resort to spelling unless the controller asks for it. For a more detailed explanation, see *Radio Mastery for VFR Pilots*, p.49.

13. "Taxi via Alpha, Echo and Papa."

_____ "Taxi via A, E, P."

Incorrect. Correct readback: "Taxi via Alpha, Echo and Papa."

14. "Maintain VFR and say your intended cruise altitude."

_____ "We'll be cruising at four thousand fife hundred."

Correct.

Note: There is no requirement to repeat "Maintain VFR."

Call signs:

The AIM has very specific guidance about how you should identify yourself on the radio, but most pilots don't follow the guidance correctly. For example, a pilot flying a Cessna Skyhawk with a registration number of N338DM might modify his call sign to 338DM, dropping the prefix. You might also hear this pilot reply to ATC by using only DM.

The AIM clearly states you should always include the prefix letter of your aircraft's registration number, in our example "N" when making a radio transmission. The AIM also says a pilot may drop the prefix and use his aircraft's make, model, or type in lieu of the prefix (AIM 4-2-4 Aircraft Call Signs).

In our example, acceptable call signs would be N338DM, Cessna 338DM, or Skyhawk 338DM. If an abbreviated call sign is used, the AIM says a pilot should continue to include the registration prefix, or the aircraft's make, model, or type, plus the last 3 numbers and digits of the aircraft's registration: N8DM, Cessna 8DM, Skyhawk 8DM.

In the following exercise, I'm going to give you an aircraft's make, model, type and registration number. Use that information to form the following:

- Three full call signs that conform to the standards in the Aeronautical Information Manual and

- 2 abbreviated versions of a call sign for that aircraft.

In the answer sections for this exercise, I'll present all of the possibilities. You only need to write 5.

Note: When including individual letters in the call sign, write the applicable letter(s) and then say the call sign out loud by speaking the letters using the phonetic pronunciation. For example, if a call sign begins with an N, write N and say "November" out loud when speaking the call sign. If a call sign ends with a T, write T and say "Tango" out loud.

1. Make: Cessna

Model: Skyhawk

Type: Single-engine

Registration: N531UC

Full call sign 1: _Skyhawk N531UC_

Full call sign 2: _Cessna 531UC_

Full call sign 3: _Skyhawk N531UC_

Abbreviated call sign 1: _Cessna 1UC_

Abbreviated call sign 2: _Skyhawk 1UC_

" 3: _N1UC_

↓↓ANSWER↓↓

Full callsign 1: N531UC. Spoken "November Fife Tree One Uniform Charlie."

Full callsign 2: Cessna 531UC. Spoken "Cessna Fife Tree One Uniform Charlie."

Full callsign 3: Skyhawk 531UC. Spoken "Skyhawk Fife Tree One Uniform Charlie."

Abbreviated callsign 1: Cessna 1UC. Spoken "Cessna One Uniform Charlie."

Abbreviated callsign 2: Skyhawk 1UC. Spoken "Skyhawk One Uniform Charlie."

Abbreviated callsign 3: N1UC. Spoken "November One Uniform Charlie."

2. Make: Piper

Model: Warrior

Type: Single-engine

Registration: N9076S

Full call sign 1: _Piper 9076S_

Full call sign 2: _Warrior 9076S_

Full call sign 3: _N9076S_

Abbreviated call sign 1: _Piper 76S_

Abbreviated call sign 2: _Warrior 76S_

_N76S_

↓↓ANSWER↓↓

Full callsign 1: N9076S. Spoken "November Niner Zero Seven Six Sierra."

Full callsign 2: Piper 9076S. Spoken "Piper Niner Zero Seven Six Sierra."

Full callsign 3: Warrior 9076S. Spoken "Warrior Niner Zero Seven Six Sierra."

Abbreviated callsign 1: Piper 76S. Spoken "Piper Seven Six Sierra."

Abbreviated callsign 2: Warrior 76S. Spoken "Warrior Seven Six Sierra."

Abbreviated callsign 3: N76S. Spoken "November Seven Six Sierra."

3. Make: Cessna

Model: Conquest

Type: Twin-engine

Registration: N311GL

Full call sign 1: _N311GL_

Full call sign 2: _Twin Cessna 311GL_

Full call sign 3: _Conquest 311GL_

Abbreviated call sign 1: _N1GL_

Abbreviated call sign 2: _Cessna 1GL_

Conquest 1GL

↓↓ANSWER↓↓

Full callsign 1: N311GL. Spoken "November Tree One One Golf Lima."

Full callsign 2: Twin Cessna 311GL. Spoken "Twin Cessna Tree One One Golf Lima."

Full callsign 3: Cessna 311GL. Spoken "Cessna Tree One One Golf Lima."

Full callsign 4: Conquest 311GL. Spoken "Conquest Tree One One Golf Lima."

Abbreviated callsign 1: Twin Cessna 1GL. Spoken "Twin Cessna One Golf Lima."

Abbreviated callsign 2: Conquest 1GL. Spoken "Conquest One Golf Lima."

Abbreviated callsign 3: Cessna 1GL. Spoken "Cessna One Golf Lima."

Abbreviated callsign 4: N1GL. Spoken "November One Golf Lima."

4. Make: Beechcraft

Model: Baron

Type: Twin-engine

Registration: N583NA _N583NA_

Full call sign 1: _BEECHCRAFT 583NA_

Full call sign 2: _BEECHCRAFT TWIN 583NA_

Full call sign 3: _BARON 583NA_

Abbreviated call sign 1: _TWIN BECHCRAFT 3NA_

Abbreviated call sign 2: _BEECHCRAFT 3NA_

TWIN BEECH BARON 3NA

_N3NA_

↓↓ANSWER↓↓

Full callsign 1: N583NA. Spoken "November Fife Eight Tree November Alpha."

Full callsign 2: Twin Beech 583NA. Spoken "Twin Beech Fife Eight Tree November Alpha."

Full callsign 3: Beech 583NA. Spoken "Beech Fife Eight Tree November Alpha."

Full callsign 4: Baron 583NA. Spoken "Baron Fife Eight Tree November Alpha."

Abbreviated callsign 1: Twin Beech 3NA. Spoken "Twin Beech Tree November Alpha."

Abbreviated callsign 2: Beech 3NA. Spoken "Beech Tree November Alpha."

Abbreviated callsign 3: Baron 3NA. Spoken "Baron Tree November Alpha."

Abbreviated callsign 4: N3NA. Spoken "November Tree November Alpha."

5. Make: Lancair

Model: Experimental

Type: Single-engine

Registration: N7249W

Full call sign 1: _N7249W_

Full call sign 2: _LANCAIR 7249W_

Full call sign 3: _EXPERIMENTAL 7249W_

Abbreviated call sign 1: _N49W_

Abbreviated call sign 2: _LANCAIR 49W_

EXPERIMENTAL 49W

↓↓ANSWER↓↓

Full callsign 1: N7249W. Spoken "November Seven Two Four Niner Whiskey."

Full callsign 2: Experimental 7249W. Spoken "Experimental Seven Two Four Niner Whiskey."

Full callsign 3: Lancair 7249W. Spoken "Lancair Seven Two Four Niner Whiskey."

Abbreviated callsign 1: Lancair 49W. Spoken "Lancair Four Niner Whiskey."

Abbreviated callsign 2: Experimental 49W. Spoken "Experimental Four Niner Whiskey."

Abbreviated callsign 3: N49W. Spoken "November Four Niner Whiskey."

6. Make: Cessna

Model: Skycatcher

Type: Light Sport

Registration: N2073X

Full call sign 1: _N2073X_

Full call sign 2: _CESSNA 2073X_

Full call sign 3: _SKY CATCHER 2073X_

Abbreviated call sign 1: _N73X_

Abbreviated call sign 2: _CESSNA 73X_

SKY CATCHER 73X

LIGHT SPORT 73X **↓↓ANSWER↓↓**

Full callsign 1: N2073X. Spoken "November Two Zero Seven Tree Xray."

Full callsign 2: Light Sport 2073X. Spoken "Light Sport Two Zero Seven Tree Xray."

Full callsign 3: Skycatcher 2073X. Spoken "Skycatcher Two Zero Seven Tree Xray."

Full callsign 4: Cessna 2073X. Spoken "Cessna Two Zero Seven Tree Xray."

Abbreviated callsign 1: Light Sport 73X. Spoken "Light Sport Seven Tree Xray."

Abbreviated callsign 2: Skycatcher 73X. Spoken "Skycatcher Seven Tree Xray."

Abbreviated callsign 3: N73X. Spoken "November Seven Tree Xray."

Abbreviated callsign 4: Cessna 73X. Spoken "Cessna Seven Tree Xray."

Uncontrolled Airport Operations

Your aircraft call sign is Cessna Niner One Tree Zero Delta (9130D). You will be departing from Atlanta Town and Country Airport (KATC), a fictitious airport on the west side of Atlanta. The airport has two runways. Runway 18/36 is 4,500 feet long. Runway 9/27 is 3,200 feet long. Each runway has a parallel taxiway. There are two parking areas at the airport. The North Ramp parking area lies to the west of Runway 18/36 at the north end of the airport. The South Ramp parking area also lies to the west of Runway 18/36 at the south end of the airport. You are currently parked on the South Ramp. (See the airport diagram for Atlanta Town and Country Airport.)

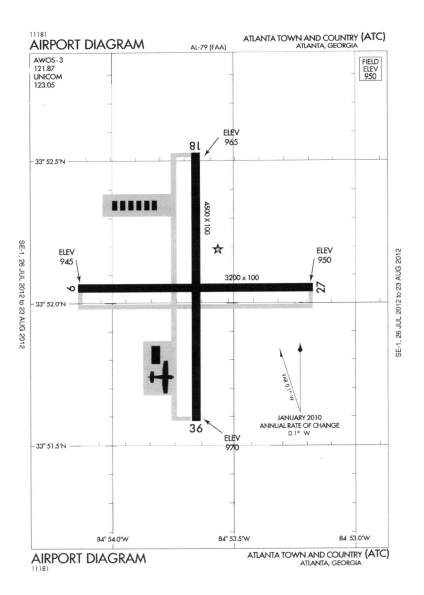

You tune the frequency for KATC's Automated Weather Observation System (AWOS) and hear the following recording on the radio:

> "Atlanta Town and Country Airport automated weather, one seven fife fife Zulu. Sky condition clear. Visibility seven miles. Wind one seven zero at one two knots. Temperature two one. Dewpoint one fife. Altimeter two niner eight seven."

Next, you tune your radio to the airport's UNICOM frequency, 123.05, and prepare to call for an airport advisory.

1. Using the airport's commonly used name of Town and Country, write the radio call you will make to get an airport advisory:

_____

_____

↓↓**ANSWER**↓↓

"Town and Country Unicom, Cessna 9130D, with the numbers, request an airport advisory." (AIM 4-1-9 e.)

Now, say it out loud:

The person manning the UNICOM frequency says, "Town and Country is using Runway One Eight with left traffic. There are currently 2 aircraft in the pattern."

2. When making any self-announce radio call in an uncontrolled airport pattern, what should you always say immediately prior to saying your call sign?

Town + Country Traffic
_____

↓↓**ANSWER**↓↓

Always say the name of the airport, plus "traffic". (AIM 4-1-9 g. 6.)

3. When making any self-announce radio call in an uncontrolled airport pattern, what should you always say immediately after you say your position in the airport pattern?

Town + Country
_____

↓↓**ANSWER**↓↓

Always say the name of the airport. (AIM 4-1-9 g. 6.)

4. After starting your aircraft's engine, what is the next radio call you would make on UNICOM?

_____

_____

↓↓**ANSWER**↓↓

"Town and Country Traffic, Cessna 9130D, taxiing to Runway One Eight from the South Ramp." (AIM TBL 4-1-1.)

What would the engine sound like at this phase of flight? Close your eyes and visualize the view you would have out of the cockpit's front windscreen. Visualize the situation and imagine the engine noise.

🎧 Now, say it out loud:

5. After taxiing out to Runway 18, and holding short of the runway, you perform your engine run-up check. You are ready to take the runway. Your intention is to remain in the airport traffic pattern for touch-and-goes. <u>When</u> do you make your next radio call?

_____

↓↓**ANSWER**↓↓

Just prior to entering the runway for takeoff.

6. Write that radio call:

Town + CounTRy TRAffic CessnA 1930 D DepaRTing RunwAy
RemAining in THe PATTeRn
18 Town + CounTRy

↓↓**ANSWER**↓↓

"Town and Country Traffic, Cessna 9130D, departing Runway One Eight, remaining in the pattern." (AIM TBL 4-1-1.)

What would the engine sound like at this phase of flight? Close your eyes and visualize the view you would have out of the cockpit's front windscreen. Visualize the situation and imagine the engine noise.

Now, say it out loud:

7. You are now flying the crosswind leg of the airport's traffic pattern. When do you make your next radio call?

_____

↓↓ANSWER↓↓

The next radio call is made as you enter the downwind leg. (AIM TBL 4-1-1.)

8. Write out that radio call:

Town + Country TRAFFic Cessna 1930D ENTERING THE Downwind
Touch +Go
Ronway 18 Town + Country

↓↓ANSWER↓↓

"Town and Country Traffic, Cessna 9130D, downwind, Runway One Eight touch-and-go, Town and Country."

What would the engine sound like at this phase of flight? Close your eyes and visualize the view you would have out of the cockpit's front windscreen. Visualize the situation and imagine the engine noise.

Now, say it out loud:

9. You are now flying the downwind leg of the airport's traffic pattern. When do you make your next radio call?

_____

↓↓ANSWER↓↓

The next radio call is made entering the base leg.

10. Write out that radio call:

Town + Country Traffic Cessna 9130 D Entering Lt base Runway 18 Touch + Go Town + Country

"Town and Country Traffic, Cessna 9130D, base leg, Runway One Eight, touch-and-go, Town and Country." (AIM TBL 4-1-1.)

What would the engine sound like at this phase of flight? Close your eyes and visualize the view you would have out of the cockpit's front windscreen. Visualize the situation and imagine the engine noise.

Now, say it out loud:

11. You are now flying the base leg of the airport's traffic pattern. When do you make your next radio call?

The next radio call is made entering final approach.

12. Write out that radio call:

Town + Country Traffic Cessna 1930 D Entering Final Approach Runway 18 Touch + Go T + C

"Town and Country Traffic, Cessna 9130D, final, Runway One Eight, touch-and-go, Town and

Country." (AIM TBL 4-1-1.)

What would the engine sound like at this phase of flight? Close your eyes and visualize the view you would have out of the cockpit's front windscreen. Visualize the situation and imagine the engine noise.

🎧 Now, say it out loud:

You have completed a touch-and-go on Runway 18 and you have flown all the way around the pattern to the end of the base leg. As you approach final, you decide, instead of touching down on the runway this time, you will practice a go-around/rejected landing.

13. What is your radio call as you enter final?

T+C TRAFFIC CESSNA 1930 D FINAL RUNWAY 18 LOW APPROACH

T+C

↓↓ANSWER↓↓

"Town and Country Traffic, Cessna 9130D, final, Runway One Eight, low approach, Town and Country." (AIM TBL 4-1-1.)

What would the engine sound like as you turn toward final approach but before beginning your go-around? Close your eyes and visualize the view you would have out of the cockpit's front windscreen. Visualize the situation and imagine the engine noise.

🎧 Now, say it out loud:

You have completed your practice go-around and now you would like to land, stop on the runway, and then takeoff in the remaining runway.

14. What is your radio call as enter base leg?

T+C TRAFFIC CESSNA 1930D LT BASS RUNWAY 18 STOP

+GO T+C

↓↓ANSWER↓↓

"Town and Country Traffic, Cessna 9130D, base leg, Runway One Eight, stop and go, Town and Country." (AIM TBL 4-1-1.)

What would the engine sound like at this phase of flight? Close your eyes and visualize the view you would have out of the cockpit's front windscreen. Visualize the situation and imagine the engine noise.

🎧 Now, say it out loud:

15. Still planning to stop on the runway and then make a takeoff on the remaining runway, what is your radio call as you enter final approach for the runway?

T+C TRAFFIC CESSNA 1930D FINAL RUNWAY 18 STOP + GO T+C

⬇⬇**ANSWER**⬇⬇

"Town and Country Traffic, Cessna 9130D, final, Runway One Eight, stop and go. Town and Country." (AIM TBL 4-1-1.)

What would the engine sound like at this phase of flight? Close your eyes and visualize the view you would have out of the cockpit's front windscreen. Visualize the situation and imagine the engine noise.

🎧 Now, say it out loud:

You are flying on crosswind leg for Runway 18. The person manning the UNICOM frequency for airport advisories announces, "Attention all aircraft in the Town and Country traffic pattern, the wind has shifted. Current winds are tree tree zero at one fife. Town and Country is now landing Runway Tree Six, left traffic. I repeat, winds are tree zero zero at one fife. Town and Country is now landing Runway Tree Six, left traffic. The new altimeter is 29.85."

16. Considering you are set up on left crosswind for Runway 18 and the airport is now using left traffic for Runway 36, what is your next radio call on UNICOM?

T+C TRAFFIC CESSNA 9130D DEPARTING the TRAFFIC PATTERN T THE EAST T+C

⬇⬇**ANSWER**⬇⬇

"Town and Country Traffic, Cessna 9130D, departing the traffic pattern to the east, Town and Country."

Explanation: From your original position on crosswind leg for Runway 18, you are on the wrong side of the runway for a left-hand pattern for Runway 36. Your best option is to depart the Runway 18 traffic pattern and re-enter at the downwind entry point for Runway 36. (See illustration.)

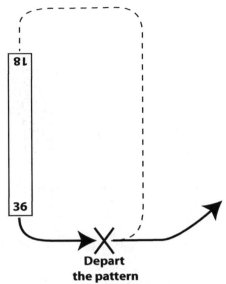

Breaking out of the pattern for Runway 18

What would the engine sound like at this phase of flight? Close your eyes and visualize the view you would have out of the cockpit's front windscreen. Visualize the situation and imagine the engine noise.

🎧 Now, say it out loud:

17. What is your next radio call as you enter the traffic pattern for Runway 36?

T+C TRAFFIC Cessna 9130D ENTERING LT DOWNWIND

Rorways 36   T+C

↓↓ANSWER↓↓

"Town and Country Traffic, Cessna 9130D, entering downwind, Runway Tree Six, Town and Country."

What would the engine sound like at this phase of flight? Close your eyes and visualize the view you would have out of the cockpit's front windscreen. Visualize the situation and imagine the engine noise.

🎧 Now, say it out loud:

Sights and Sounds Questions

The following exercises should increase your awareness of the sights and sounds within your aircraft cockpit when making various radio calls. Here are some radio calls you might make while in the Atlanta Town and Country Airport's uncontrolled traffic pattern. After reading each of these calls out loud, answer the following questions below each radio call.

"Town and Country Traffic, Cessna Niner One Tree Zero Delta, downwind, Runway One Eight, touch-and-go, Town and Country." (Made when entering the downwind leg.)

1. At what clock position (for example 12 o'clock), relative to the nose of your aircraft, would the active runway be when you make this radio call?

_____10_____ o'clock.

↓↓ANSWER↓↓

10 o'clock. (See illustration.)

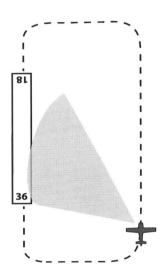

2. When making the above radio call, would the sound of your aircraft engine be:

 a) high RPM. b) medium RPM. c) low RPM.

↓↓ANSWER↓↓

b.) Medium RPM if at pattern altitude. High RPM if still climbing to pattern altitude.

"Town and Country Traffic, Cessna Niner One Tree Zero Delta, base leg, Runway One Eight, touch-and-go, Town and Country."

Assume your aircraft has a front windscreen divided into left and right sections, and a front window and back window on each side of the aircraft, and no rear window. In which windscreen section or window would the runway appear when you make the above radio call?

3. The _____ Lt FRONT wiNDow _____

↓↓**ANSWER**↓↓

Front left window. (See illustration.)

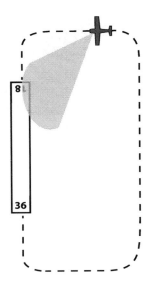

4. Would the sound of your aircraft engine be:

a) high RPM. b) medium RPM. c) low RPM.

↓↓**ANSWER**↓↓

c) low RPM.

"Town and Country Traffic, Cessna Niner One Tree Zero Delta, entering downwind, Runway One Eight, Town and Country."

5. Assume you make this radio call just prior to entering the left downwind at midfield, from outside the traffic pattern, and your entry is at a 45-degree angle to downwind. At what clock position would the runway be, relative to the nose of your aircraft, when you make this radio call?

_____ o'clock.

↓↓ANSWER↓↓

10 to 11 o'clock. (See illustration.)

6. Recall the situation I described earlier: You were on a left crosswind leg for Runway 18 when the airport advisory service announced the airport was switching to Runway 36. You'll remember you had to break out of the pattern for Runway 18 and re-enter at the midfield downwind entry point for Runway 36, for a left-hand traffic pattern. Just prior to making the radio call announcing your intention to enter the traffic pattern for Runway 36, what is the clock position of the runway relative to the nose of your aircraft?

_____ o'clock.

↓↓ANSWER↓↓

10 to 11 o'clock—the same clock position as the entry for Runway 18.

7. You have completed your planned pattern work at Atlanta Town and Country Airport and you are planning to depart the airport pattern. Acceptable departure routes from the airport include straight out, 45-degree exit, or departure from the crosswind leg. Assuming you have just completed a touch-and-go on Runway 36, and you wish to depart to the northwest, what would be your next radio call?

T+C TRAFFIC CESSNA 9130D DEPARTING PATTERN TO

THE NW T+C

"Town and Country Traffic, Cessna 9130D, departing to the northwest, Town and County."

What would the engine sound like at this phase of flight? Close your eyes and visualize the view you would have out of the cockpit's front windscreen. Visualize the situation and imagine the engine noise.

🎧 Now, say it out loud:

8. Where would the runway be, in clock position relative to the nose of your aircraft, when you make this radio call?

_____ o'clock.

↓↓**ANSWER**↓↓

---

8 o'clock. You would use the 45-degree exit from the takeoff leg to depart northwest. (See illustration.)

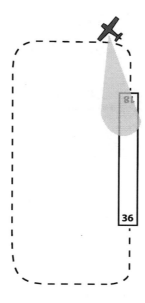

9. When exiting the airport traffic pattern, according the recommendation in the AIM, until how many miles

from the airport should you keep your radio tuned to the airport's traffic advisory frequency?

_____10_____ miles.

↓↓**ANSWER**↓↓

10 miles, unless Consolidated Federal Regulations (CFR) or local area procedures dictate otherwise. (AIM 4-1-9 c. 1.)

10. Why should you keep your radio tuned to the airport's traffic advisory frequency until the recommended distance from the airport?

_____

_____

↓↓**ANSWER**↓↓

To listen for any position reports from traffic around the airport that may cross your path.

11. You are 15 miles west of the Town and Country Airport. The person manning the airport advisory position has told you the airport is using Runway 18 and there is one aircraft already in the traffic pattern.

When would you make your first self-announce radio call on Town and Country's UNICOM frequency?

_____

↓↓**ANSWER**↓↓

10 miles out from the airport. (AIM TBL 4-1-1.)

12. Write the radio call you would make at that point:

T+C TRAFFIC CESSNA 9/800 10 miles WEST FUR LANDING

will Be using Runway 18

42

"Town and Country Traffic, Cessna 9130D, one zero miles west of the airport, inbound for landing, Town and Country."

What would the engine sound like at this phase of flight? Close your eyes and visualize the view you would have out of the cockpit's front windscreen. Visualize the situation and imagine the engine noise.

🎧 Now, say it out loud:

Situational Awareness in an Uncontrolled Airport Traffic Pattern

You are flying on the crosswind leg for Runway 36, using a left pattern. You hear the following radio call from another airplane: "Town and Country Traffic, Piper Seven Zero Two Echo Charlie, downwind, Runway 36, Town and Country."

1. Assume your airplane's front windscreen is divided into a left and right section, and your airplane has two front side windows and two rear side windows, but no rear window. When you hear the above radio call, in which window would you expect to see Piper 702EC?

Left windscreen.

Right windscreen.

Front left window.

Front right window.

Rear left window.

Rear right window.

Not in sight, at your 6 o'clock position.

↓↓ANSWER↓↓

Front left window or left windscreen, depending on how far each aircraft has traveled on its respective leg of the traffic pattern.

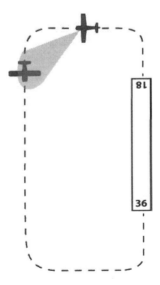

2. You have just initiated your turn from takeoff leg to crosswind leg in a left-hand pattern for Runway 36. You hear the following radio call from another aircraft: "Town and Country Traffic, Cirrus Four Seven Niner Sierra Zulu, base leg, Runway 36, Town and Country."

When you hear the above radio call, in which window would you expect to see Cirrus 479SZ?

Left windscreen.

Right windscreen.

Front left window.

Front right window.

Rear left window.

Rear right window.

Not in sight, at your 6 o'clock position.

↓↓**ANSWER**↓↓

Rear left window.

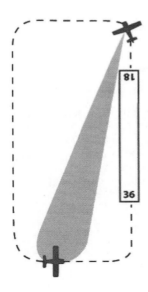

3. You are on downwind leg, left-hand pattern for Runway 36. You have not quite reached the turn for base leg. You hear the following radio call from another aircraft: "Town and Country Traffic, Mooney Six Zero Six Kilo Mike, downwind, Runway 36, Town and Country."

When you hear the above radio call, in which window would you expect to see Mooney 606KM?

Left windscreen.

Right windscreen.

Front left window.

Front right window.

Rear left window.

Rear right window.

Not in sight, at your 6 o'clock position.

↓↓**ANSWER** ↓↓

Not in sight, at your 6 o'clock position.

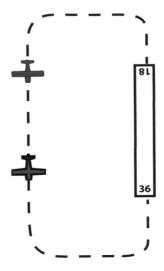

4. You are on downwind leg in the left-hand pattern for Runway 36, approaching base leg. You hear the following radio call from another aircraft: "Town and Country Traffic, Twin Cessna Tree Eight Six Whiskey Victor, fife miles west of the airport, Runway 36, Town and Country."

When you hear the above radio call, in which window would you expect to see Twin Cessna 386WV?

Left windscreen.

Right windscreen.

Front left window.

Front right window.

Rear left window.

Rear right window.

↓↓**ANSWER**↓↓

Rear right window.

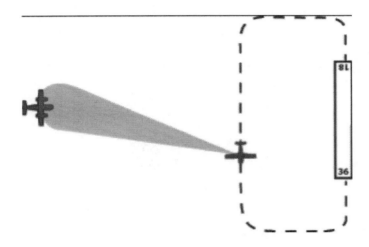

5. Bonus Questions: Did Twin Cessna 386WV just make a mandatory radio call, according to the AIM?

Yes.   No.

↓↓**ANSWER**↓↓

No. However, there is nothing in the AIM that prohibits a pilot from making this call. In some cases, it might be prudent, as a technique to make extra position reports. Sometimes, a timely position report, even one made in a non-standard location, can help another aircraft remain clear of your flight path. For more on radio techniques in an uncontrolled airport pattern, see *Radio Mastery for VFR Pilots*, Chapter 5.

VFR Flight Following with an Air Route Traffic Control Center (ARTCC)

Which of the following statements are true about VFR flight following? Check each item that is true:

1. ___ It is free service offered to any pilot flying an aircraft with an operable transponder (Mode C not required) and a communication radio.

2. ___ It offers a bird's eye view of air traffic you may not spot from your airplane.

3. ___ It can provide recommended headings that will steer your aircraft safely around conflicting traffic.

4. ___ It can warn you of airspace ahead that you are not allowed to enter, such as active warning areas, restricted areas, prohibited areas, and temporary flight restriction areas.

5. ___ It can provide safety alerts when you fly your aircraft too close to terrain.

6. ___ It can provide recommended headings to navigation points and destinations upon request.

7. ___ ATC will point out areas of precipitation along your route of flight.

8. ___ Workload permitting, ATC will fetch weather information for your intended destination, upon request.

9. ___ ATC offers immediate assistance in an emergency.

10. ___ You are not required to follow any of ATC's recommendations while you are using VFR flight following.

11. ___ You are not restricted by ATC from flying where and when you wish to fly while using VFR flight following, as long as you remain clear of active warning areas, restricted areas, prohibited areas, and temporary flight restriction areas.

↓↓ANSWER↓↓

1 – 11. All of the statements are true. The only additional effort you have to make, when using VFR flight following, is to keep ATC advised of any altitude changes you plan to make. That's it!

With this in mind, answer these questions. Assume you are using VFR flight following in each of the following situations:

12. Will ATC allow you to fly into an active Military Operating Area?

 Yes. No. Maybe.

↓↓ANSWER↓↓

Yes. ATC cannot restrict you from entering an active MOA if you are operating under VFR. However, expect ATC to strongly discourage you from entering due to the extreme risk of a midair collision with a military aircraft flying in the MOA. (AIM 3-4-5 c. Military Operating Areas. *Radio Mastery for VFR Pilots*, Chapter 7, p. 117.)

13. When ATC says, "Traffic, 12 o'clock, opposite direction, 5 miles, same altitude. For traffic avoidance, suggest you turn left, heading zero fife zero," are you required to fly that heading for traffic avoidance?

Yes. No. Maybe.

↓↓ANSWER↓↓

No. However, I strongly recommend complying with ATC's recommended heading unless you have a compelling reason not to do so. (AIM 4-1-15 b. 2.)

14. If you ask ATC to give you a heading to fly that will steer you towards a navaid or airport, and that heading will put your aircraft closer to clouds than allowed by Visual Flight Rules, are you required to maintain that heading?

Yes. No. Maybe.

↓↓ANSWER↓↓

No. You are not required to maintain ATC's recommended heading. You should not maintain any heading that would put you closer to clouds than allowed by VFR. (AIM 5-5-6 Pilot/Controller Responsibilities a. 3.)

15. When ATC gives you a heading to fly direct to a navaid or to an airport, is that heading corrected for known winds aloft?

Yes. No. Maybe.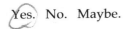

↓↓**ANSWER**↓↓

Yes. The headings ATC provides are wind-corrected based upon the latest winds aloft information. The wind information ATC uses will be based either on forecasted winds aloft or based upon winds aloft reports given by pilots.

16. When crossing over from one ARTCC sector to the next, while in radar contact, do you have to initialize contact with the controller in the next sector, i.e., give that new controller your position and obtain a new transponder code?

Yes. No. Maybe.

↓↓**ANSWER**↓↓

No. If your airplane is in radar contact, the new controller will have your aircraft identified and located on his radar display even before you check in with him on the radio.

17. When crossing over from an ARTCC sector to the airspace of Approach Control for an airport, do you have to initialize contact with the approach controller, i.e., give the approach controller your position and obtain a new transponder code?

Yes. No. Maybe.

↓↓**ANSWER**↓↓

No. ARTCC controllers will give a positive handoff of your aircraft to an approach control, just as they do when handing your aircraft off from sector to sector. However, the approach controller may assign a new transponder code to your aircraft to better fit it into his radar system. (AIM 4-2-3 Contact Procedures.)

18. Can the controller at an ARTCC give you precise headings that will ensure you avoid all precipitation along your route of flight?

Yes. No. Maybe.

↓↓**ANSWER**↓↓

No. At present, ARTCC radar only allows depiction of very generalized areas of precipitation. Precise vectors around these areas are not possible. (AIM 7-1-14 ATC Inflight Weather Avoidance.)

19. Can the controller at an ARTCC give you precise headings that will ensure your aircraft maintains the minimum VFR inflight visibility for the airspace in which you are flying?

Yes. No. Maybe.

↓↓**ANSWER**↓↓

No. An ARTCC controller can only refer to surface depiction maps to determine general areas of VFR and marginal VFR. He has no other source to help you maintain VFR inflight visibility minimums.

20. In the space below, list as many types of assistance you think ATC can provide for you when you declare an emergency. For example, activating airport rescue and fire fighting service at your intended destination is one type of assistance. (My list of answers is on the next page.)

This is my list. You may have additional items in your list. An exact match with my list is not required:

- Clear all other aircraft in contact with ATC out of your way to give you priority for landing at an airport.

- Clear all other aircraft in contact with ATC out of your way as you perform inflight control and stability checks.

- Provide a list of nearby runways, and all of the information you might need about the characteristics of those runways.

- Provide a list of nearby airports, and all of the information you might need about the services available at those airports.

- Get weather updates.

- Relay any information you need to pass to, or receive from, other agencies, businesses, or individuals.

- Coordinate for paramedics to meet your aircraft upon arrival.

- Coordinate airport fire and rescue services to meet your aircraft upon arrival.

- Coordinate police or other law enforcement agencies to meet your aircraft upon arrival.

- Provide vectors towards any airport or area you request.

- Provide information about usable navaids in your area.

- Make suggestions, when requested, to help you cope with your emergency.

VFR Flight Following Radio Calls

Your call sign is Cessna 9130D. You have just departed the traffic pattern at Atlanta Town and Country Airport and you would like to pick up VFR Flight Following service from the overlying ARTCC, Atlanta Center. You are currently climbing through 3,000 feet with a planned cruising altitude of 6,500 feet. Your destination is the Pryor Regional Airport in Decatur, Alabama. The airport is approximately 100 nautical miles northwest of your present position.

For initial check-in with any air traffic control agency, we use the meme: *You. Me. Where. What.* Let's break that down:

You: Who you are calling. Include the name of the ATC facility and the type of facility. For example, New York Approach; Van Nuys Ground; Palm Beach Departure; Gainesville Tower; Oakland Center.

Me: Your full call sign.

Where: Your position over the ground and your altitude. Position can be expressed as a known landmark, an approximate bearing and distance from a navaid or airport, a precise radial and DME from a VORTAC, or VOR/DME. Altitude is your current altitude, plus the altitude at which you intend to level off if you are climbing or descending.

What: Your situation or your request, if applicable, <u>in a very brief statement</u>. Examples: "VFR," "Request flight following," "Emergency".

There is an extensive discussion of procedures and techniques for making initial contact with ATC in *Radio Mastery for VFR Pilots*, Chapter 7.

1. In the meme *You, Me, Where, What*, why is it so important to always state the name of the ATC facility you are trying to contact when making your initial call to that facility?

↓↓ANSWER↓↓

To ensure you are talking to the correct ATC agency. (AIM 4-2-3 a. Initial Contact.)

Your initial check-in with a new controller gets modified if your aircraft is currently in radar contact. You still use the meme You, Me, Where, What. The "Where" portion of your statement does not require you to state your position over the ground. Your position will already be known to ATC thanks to radar contact. All you need to say in the "Where" portion is your altitude and the altitude you are targeting for level-off if you are climbing or descending.

Let's plug You, Me, Where, What into some questions. For each of the following questions, assume your aircraft is <u>not</u> in radar contact and you would like to pick up VFR flight following. In all cases, your call sign will be Cessna 9130D.

You have just departed the Atlanta Town and Country Airport, flying to the northwest. You intend to fly to your destination of Pryor Regional Airport in Decatur, Alabama. Pryor Regional is another uncontrolled airport. Here are your instrument panel readings as you check in with Atlanta Center for flight following:

Heading: 310 degrees.

Airspeed: 85 knots.

Altitude: 4,200.

Vertical Speed: 500 fpm climb.

Town and Country VOR radial: 315.

Town and Country DME: 15.

Your intended cruising altitude is: 6,500.

2. Write the initial radio call you would make to the center controller to pick up VFR flight following, remembering to use the format You, Me, Where, What:

Atlanta Center Traffic Cessna 9130D 15 miles

Northwest of The T+C Vor, VFR

↓↓ANSWER↓↓

"Atlanta Center, Cessna 9130D, one fife miles northwest of the Town and Country VOR, VFR (or, request VFR flight following)." (AIM 4-2-3 a. Initial Contact.)

What would the engine sound like at this phase of flight? Close your eyes and visualize the view you would have out of the cockpit's front windscreen. Visualize the situation and imagine the engine noise.

Now, say it out loud:

Explanation: I baited you with all of the extra flight parameters in this scenario. Remember, when making initial contact with ATC, keep your first radio call short and simple.

You are flying VFR southeast along the V-120 airway between Lewistown and Miles City, Montana. Your cruising altitude is 5,500. Your cruising airspeed is 130 knots indicated. Your destination is the Aberdeen Regional Airport, South Dakota. You would like to pick up flight following with an enroute center (ARTCC).

3. Where could you look to find out the name and frequency of the enroute center you should contact?

↓↓ANSWER↓↓

On an enroute low altitude chart in the postage stamp box nearest your location.

Note: Enroute low altitude charts are commonly used by pilots when flying IFR. They do not depict terrain and other surface features like sectional charts. Due to their uncluttered, white background, it is much easier to identify airways, navaids, and intersections on enroute low charts. They also provide more extensive information on enroute air traffic control, including ARTCC radio frequencies. For these reasons, I carry enroute low charts for my route of flight when flying VFR.

Look at the enroute chart below. You are currently 30 miles northeast of the Salmon VOR on V-121.

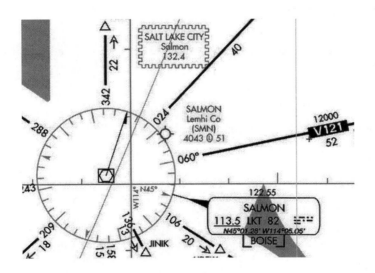

4. What is the name of the enroute center you would call?

_____.

↓↓ANSWER↓↓

Salt Lake City Center. (Commonly spoken as "Salt Lake Center.")

5. What frequency would you use to make contact?

_____.

↓↓ANSWER↓↓

132.4

6. Write the radio call to make initial contact with the enroute controller:

_____

_____

↓↓ANSWER↓↓

"Salt Lake City Center, Cessna 9130D, tree zero northeast of Salmon, VFR." (AIM 4-2-3 a. Initial Contact.)

What would the engine sound like at this phase of flight? Close your eyes and visualize the view you would have out of the cockpit's front windscreen. Visualize the situation and imagine the engine noise.

Now, say it out loud:

You have just departed the traffic pattern at Garrett County Airport, Maryland. Your plan is to accomplish practice airwork—stalls, steep turns, etc.--in the general area 20 miles north of the airport. You are currently climbing through 3,200 feet to an initial cruising altitude of 4,500 feet. You plan to do your airwork between 3,000 and 5,000 feet MSL. While working, you would like to stay in contact with Cleveland Center. By staying in contact with Cleveland Center, the controller can watch out for traffic conflicts while you practice.

7. Write the radio call to make initial contact with Cleveland Center:

_____

_____

↓↓ANSWER↓↓

"Cleveland Center, Cessna 9130D, off Garrett County, request VFR flight following." Or, "Cleveland Center, 9130D, XX miles north of Garrett County, VFR." (AIM 4-2-3 a. Initial Contact.)

What would the engine sound like at this phase of flight? Close your eyes and visualize the view you would have out of the cockpit's front windscreen. Visualize the situation and imagine the engine noise.

Now, say it out loud:

Explanation: Again, keep the initial radio simple. You can explain what you need after the controller assigns a transponder code to you and asks you for your request.

It is a beautiful fall day. You have 3 friends with you onboard your aircraft. They are along for a ride to look at the fall leaf colors over Central New Hampshire. You are currently 15 miles south of the Lebanon VORTAC at 3,500 feet MSL. Your plan is to cruise over the hills between 3,000 and 4,000 feet MSL. You would like to pick up flight following with Boston Center as you weave back and forth over the hills.

8. Write the radio call to make initial contact with Boston Center:

_____

_____

↓↓ANSWER↓↓

"Boston Center, Cessna 9130D, one fife miles south of the Lebanon VORTAC, requesting VFR flight following." (AIM 4-2-3 a. Initial Contact.)

What would the engine sound like at this phase of flight? Close your eyes and imagine the view you would have out of the cockpit's front windscreen. Visualize the situation and imagine the engine noise.

🎧 Now, say it out loud:

You are doing practice airwork over the flatlands southeast of Roswell, New Mexico. Suddenly, your aircraft engine starts running rough and you notice the smell of burning oil. You do some troubleshooting but the engine sounds even worse and you can now see a little smoke in the cockpit. There is no doubt you are in an emergency situation. You tune in the Chisum VORTAC, which is just northwest of the Roswell International Airport, and notice you are on the Chisum 120-degree radial at 40 DME.

Although you were not in contact with ATC, you decide you had better get in contact and get some emergency assistance. You dial in Albuquerque Center on your Number 1 Comm Radio as you turn toward the Chisum VORTAC.

9. Write the radio call to make initial contact with Albuquerque Center:

_____

_____

↓↓ANSWER↓↓

"Albuquerque Center, Cessna 9130D, four zero miles southeast of the Chisum VORTAC, declaring an emergency." (AIM 4-2-3 a. Initial Contact.)

Close your eyes and imagine the sound and feel of this rough-running engine. Visualize the scene you would have out of the cockpit's front windscreen.

🎧 Now, say it out loud:

Explanation: This is one of those situations in which it would be tempting to go into detail on your first radio call: "I have smoke in the cockpit. My engine is running rough, and I need to get on the ground ASAP!" Don't do it. If you throw all that information at the controller in your first radio call, he is going to miss most of it. Simply make contact and let the controller register your aircraft on his radar screen. After that process, you will be able to relay all of the pertinent details and be assured they are heard and understood.

What about using the word "Mayday"? We cover that extensively in a later section on emergencies. For now, know that saying "I'm declaring an emergency" will suffice.

Subsequent Radio Transmissions with an ARTCC

1. You are conducting an aerial sightseeing tour of the barrier islands around Wilmington, North Carolina. For this tour, you will be changing headings and altitudes frequently as you maneuver around the islands. You figure you will be working between 2,000 and 3,500 feet MSL

You have made initial contact with Washington Center and checked in at 3,500, for VFR flight following. The controller assigns a transponder code to your flight and says, "Say your request." Write what you would say to the controller to get flight following as you tour the islands:

_____

_____

↓↓ANSWER↓↓

Words similar to this: "Cessna 9130D will be sight-seeing around the barrier islands between 2,000 and 3,500."

Note: Some pilots are reluctant to use ATC's flight following service when flying a random flight path and making frequent altitude changes. I'd argue this is one of the most important times to use flight following. ATC can help you keep track of traffic all the way around your airplane when you are maneuvering.

What would the engine sound like at this phase of flight? Close your eyes and visualize the view you would have out of the cockpit's front windscreen. Visualize the situation and imagine the engine noise.

🎧 Now, say it out loud:

2. You have departed in your Cessna 182 from the Ocala, Florida airport. You are northbound, heading to Valdosta, Georgia. You have made initial contact with Jax Center (Jacksonville), checking in with, "Jax Center, Cessna 362NM, two zero miles north of Ocala, VFR." Write what you would say to the controller to get flight following as you proceed to Valdosta:

_____

_____

↓↓**ANSWER**↓↓

"Cessna 362NM is enroute to Valdosta, GA. We're requesting flight following."

What would the engine sound like at this phase of flight? Close your eyes and visualize the view you would have out of the cockpit's front windscreen. Visualize the situation and imagine the engine noise.

Now, say it out loud:

3. When an enroute controller says to you, "Radar contact lost," does that mean the controller is no longer providing flight following?

Circle the correct answer:

Yes. No. Maybe.

↓↓**ANSWER**↓↓

No. (AIM Pilot/Controller Glossary.)

Explanation: A controller can continue to provide a degraded level of flight following by having you make position reports. The controller will track your progress based on those reports. When not in radar contact, position reports to ATC are required when flying on an IFR flight plan. ATC can and will work with your position reports when you are flying VFR, but they are not mandatory.

4. When an enroute controller says to you, "Radar service terminated," does that mean the controller is no longer providing flight following?

Yes. No. Maybe.

↓↓**ANSWER**↓↓

Yes. (AIM Pilot/Controller Glossary.)

Explanation: The operative words are "service terminated."

Traffic Advisories from an ARTCC

1. You are flying over southern Missouri, in radar contact with Kansas City Center for VFR flight following. Kansas City says, "Piper 316YH, traffic 12 o'clock and ten miles, opposite direction, 1000 feet below you." You scan for the traffic and do not see it. Write the radio call you would make to Kansas City Center:

_____

_____

↓↓ANSWER↓↓

"Piper 316YH, negative contact." (AIM Pilot/Controller Glossary.)

Note: From this point forward, I will no longer include the instructions to close your eyes and visualize your situation while imagining the cockpit sounds. I strongly recommend you continue the visualization practice as you speak the radio transmission. Your prompt to do all three items (visualize, imagine, and speak) will continue to be,

🎧 Now, say it out loud:

2. Still with Kansas City Center, the controller says, "Piper 316YH, traffic 11 o'clock and 5 miles, southwest bound, at 4,500." You see the reported traffic. Write the radio call you would make to Kansas City Center:

_____

_____

↓↓ANSWER↓↓

"Piper 316YH, traffic in sight." (AIM Pilot/Controller Glossary.)

🎧 Now, say it out loud:

3. Still with Kansas City Center, you are cruising at 5,500 feet MSL. The controller says, "Piper 316YH, traffic 12 o'clock, 5 miles, opposite direction, Mode C indicates 5,000 climbing, unverified."

What does the controller mean when he says, "unverified"?

_____

_____

↓↓ANSWER↓↓

"Unverified" means the controller has not verified that the altitude he is reading on his radar display matches the aircraft's actual altitude. (AIM 4-1-15 Radar Traffic Information Services.)

Explanation: This is because he is not in radio contact with the pilot of that airplane and cannot ask the pilot to confirm his altitude.

4. You scan for the traffic just reported by Kansas City Center and you do not see the traffic. You reply, "Piper 316YH, negative contact." The controller replies, "Piper 316YH, for traffic avoidance, suggest a right turn, heading one two zero."

Are you required to fly the heading given to you by the controller?

Circle the correct answer:

Yes. No. Maybe.

↓↓ANSWER↓↓

No. (AIM 5-5-6 a. 3. Radar Vectors.)

Explanation: Notice the controller said, "Suggest a right turn." If you have a reason not to fly the suggested heading, you may choose an alternate course of action. Advise the controller of your intentions.

5. As you initiate a turn to the suggested right turn to 120 degrees, you make a radio call to the controller. Write what you would say to the controller:

_____

_____

↓↓**ANSWER** ↓↓

"Piper 316YH, right, heading one two zero." (AIM 5-5-2 a. 1. Air Traffic Clearance.)

🎧 Now, say it out loud:

6. You continue flight following with Kansas City Center over Southern Missouri (Class E airspace). You are entering an area of widely scattered clouds at your cruising altitude of 5,500 feet MSL. You managed to maintain VFR cloud clearances with only an occasional minor heading change.

First, what are the VFR cloud clearance minimum distances for your situation?

_____ above cloud.

_____ below cloud.

_____ laterally from cloud.

↓↓**ANSWER** ↓↓

Consolidated Federal Regulations 91.155 Basic VFR Weather Minimums:

1000 above.

500 below.

2000 laterally (Meme: 1-5-2).

7. Second, what is the minimum inflight visibility you must maintain in your current situation?

_____ miles. Is that measurement stated in *statute* or *nautical* miles? (Circle the correct measurement unit.)

↓↓**ANSWER** ↓↓

3 statute miles. (CFR 91.155)

8. Kansas City Center says, "Piper 6YH, VFR traffic 12 o'clock, 7 miles, opposite direction, type and altitude unknown."

Why would the controller say the traffic is "type and altitude unknown"?

_____

↓↓ANSWER↓↓

The controller is showing an unidentified target on his radar screen with no Mode C (altitude) information. (AIM 4-1-15 c. 2. Radar Traffic Information Service.)

9. You do not see the reported traffic. You tell the controller, "Piper 6YH, negative contact." The controller replies, "Piper 6YH, for traffic avoidance, suggest a left turn, heading zero niner zero." The suggested turn is a heading change of 40 degrees to the left. You look 40 degrees to your left and see a cumulus cloud at your altitude, about 1/2 mile away. You determine the heading given to you by Kansas City Center would cause you to fly closer to that cloud than allowed by VFR cloud clearance minimums. What do you fly--not say--in response to the controller's suggested heading, knowing the reported traffic is getting very close to your position? Remember, neither you, nor the controller, know the traffic's actual altitude.

_____

_____

↓↓ANSWER↓↓

You would make a turn to the right of 40 degrees of heading change. (This assumes the path to the right will maintain VFR cloud clearances and not violate airspace you should not be flying into.) Or, you could turn even further left, if turning more than 40 degrees would also avoid the cloud.

There is a good discussion of this scenario, along with your options, in *Radio Mastery for VFR Pilots*, Chapter 7, p. 116.

10. After initiating your 40-degree turn to the right to a new heading of one seven zero, to avoid the reported traffic, what would you say to the controller?

_____

_____

↓↓ANSWER↓↓

"Piper 6YH is turning right to one seven zero to avoid the traffic and clouds." (*Radio Mastery for VFR Pilots*, Chapter 7.)

🎧 Now, say it out loud:

Still with Kansas City Center in the same general location, the controller says, "Piper 6YH, traffic 10 o'clock, 8 miles, southwest bound, Mode C indicates 6,000, descending, unverified." You do not see the traffic and report that to the controller. The controller replies, "Piper 6YH, for traffic avoidance, suggest you turn right, heading one four zero."

In this case, clouds will not be a factor. As you respond to the controller and begin to start your turn, you spot the traffic. The traffic is a biplane below your altitude and descending. You can clearly see the biplane is no conflict with your flight path.

11. Once you have initiated your turn to the avoidance heading, do you have to complete that turn if you determine the traffic you were avoiding is no conflict with your aircraft?

Circle the correct answer:

Yes. No. Maybe.

↓↓ANSWER↓↓

No. (AIM 5-5-10 a. Traffic Advisories.)

Explanation: The controller's turn is a suggestion based upon current conditions —traffic not in sight. If you see the traffic, that condition no longer applies.

12. If you abandon your turn to avoid traffic and decide to resume your original course, write the radio call you would make to the controller:

_____

"Piper 6YH has the traffic in sight. I'm returning to course." (AIM 5-5-10 a. Traffic Advisories.)

Now, say it out loud:

Working with an ARTCC Around Restricted Airspace

You are flying VFR to the northeast, paralleling the coastline of southern Georgia. Jacksonville (Jax) Center says to you, "Mooney 5713H, you are approaching the Coastal 4 Military Operating Area. The MOA is currently hot. Would you like a vector around the MOA or can you navigate around it yourself?"

1. First, what does the controller mean when he says, "The MOA is hot"?

_____

_____

↓↓**ANSWER**↓↓

He means the MOA is in use by the military. (AIM 3-4-5 Military Operating Areas.)

2. Second, are you required to avoid flying through an active MOA when VFR?

Circle the correct answer:

Yes. No. Maybe.

↓↓**ANSWER**↓↓

No.

Explanation: When operating under VFR, you may travel through an active MOA.

3. Why does the controller not want you to fly through the MOA?

_____

_____

To avoid a collision with a military aircraft. (AIM 3-4-5 Military Operating Areas.)

Explanation: Military aircraft operating in a MOA are usually not under ATC's control. These aircraft operate at high speed and maneuver unpredictably. ATC may not be able to help steer you away from a collision with aircraft inside a MOA.

Controllers are very concerned about mixing high speed military aircraft with slower civilian aircraft. Take a look at *Radio Mastery for VFR Aircraft*, p. 117 for an interesting story about how a controller put a fighter pilot in his place for straying outside of a MOA.

4. Third, when the controller offers to vector you around the MOA, what information will he provide if you accept his offer to vector your aircraft?

_____

_____

Headings and/or altitude changes to avoid the airspace. (AIM 3-4-5 Military Operating Areas.)

Explanation: All MOAs have a base and a top. If you prefer to not fly around a MOA, you may be able to avoid the airspace by flying above the MOA top or below the MOA base. Refer to the applicable navigation chart for a MOA's base and top.

5. You are now past the Coastal 4 MOA. The controller at Jax Center says, "Mooney 5713H, Restricted Area 3007 Bravo is at your 12 o'clock and two zero miles. The restricted area is currently hot. Would you like a vector around restricted airspace, or will you navigate around it on your own?"

When VFR, are you required to avoid flying through active restricted airspace?

Circle the correct answer:

Yes. No. Maybe.

Yes. (AIM 3-4-3 Restricted Areas.)

6. If the restricted airspace is reported as inactive, are you allowed to fly through it?

Circle the correct answer:

   Yes. No. Maybe.

↓↓**ANSWER** ↓↓

Maybe. (AIM 3-4-3 Restricted Areas.)

Explanation: Some areas of restricted airspace may be flown through when inactive. Refer to the applicable navigation chart and NOTAMs for the airspace in question. If in doubt, do not fly through restricted airspace.

7. You decide to accept vectoring service from Jax Center. The controller says, "Mooney 5713H, turn right, heading zero six zero. Vectors around restricted airspace."

Write your reply to Jax Center:

_____

_____

↓↓**ANSWER** ↓↓

"Mooney 5713H, turn right, heading zero six zero." (AIM 5-5-2 a. 1. Air Traffic Clearance.)

Explanation: The controller will almost always give you a reason for a vector. This is advisory information that you do not have to repeat.

🎧 Now, say it out loud:

8. After receiving vectors from Jax Center for a few minutes, the controller says, "Mooney 13H, restricted airspace is no longer a factor. Resume own navigation on course." Write your reply to Jax Center:

_____

_____

↓↓**ANSWER** ↓↓

"Mooney 13H, returning to course." Or, "Mooney 13H, resuming own navigation."

◯ Now, say it out loud:

You are currently flying off the coast of North Carolina, over the Atlantic Ocean, heading generally south. You are not in contact with any ATC facility, but you do have your Number 2 Comm radio tuned to the universal emergency frequency of 121.5.

You are cruising at 6,500, indicating 120 knots as you fly into a 10-knot headwind. Your transponder is squawking 1200. All of a sudden you hear this in your radio headset:

"This is Giant Killer on Guard. Aircraft two zero miles northwest of the Wilmington VOR, heading one niner zero. Squawking one two zero zero. Mode C indicating six thousand, fife hundred. Approximate groundspeed of 100 knots. You are approaching an active military warning area. Turn right heading two one zero immediately and contact Wilmington Approach on 125.0."

9. Would you respond to this radio call?

Circle the correct answer:

     Yes. No. Maybe.

↓↓**ANSWER** ↓↓

Maybe. (AIM 3-4-4 Warning Areas.)

Explanation: If your flight parameters match or almost match the numbers in Giant Killer's transmission, you should comply with the directions given on the radio.

10. If you don't respond to this radio call and the aircraft described is you, what would you expect to hear next on the radio?

_____

You would hear a repeat of the information several more times. (AIM 3-4-4 Warning Areas.)

Explanation: The military radar monitor, in this case Giant Killer, would continue repeating the warning until you either turn away from the warning area, or until the military decides to take action against your aircraft.

11. If you would respond to this radio call, describe your actions:

_____

_____

You would turn to the heading indicated by Giant Killer and then contact Wilmington Approach Control on the frequency indicated.

You will receive a similar warning from a military agency on frequency 121.5 if you fly too close to a prohibited area.

12. If you choose to ignore repeated warnings, what would you expect to happen as you proceeded into the prohibited area?

_____

_____

You might be intercepted by fighter aircraft. The military transmission would also tell you to contact the fighter aircraft on frequency 121.5. (AIM 3-4-2 Prohibited Areas. 5-6-2 Interception Procedures.)

For further information on what to do when being intercepted by fighter aircraft, see a complete explanation in *Radio Mastery for VFR Pilots*, or refer to the Aeronautical Information Manual, Chapter 5.

Handoffs from an ARTCC

New day, new situation. You are flying as Beech 479TG on a Victor airway in northern Washington State. Seattle Center has your aircraft in radar contact. Your cruising altitude is 8,500 feet MSL. Your present position is 45 DME southeast of the Whatcom VORTAC. The controller at Seattle Center says, "Beechcraft 9TG, for further flight following, contact Seattle Center on 133.4."

1. Write your reply to the controller:

_____

_____

↓↓ANSWER↓↓

"Beechcraft 9TG, 133.4." (AIM 4-2-3 d. Acknowledgment of Frequency Changes.)

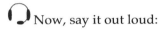 Now, say it out loud:

Explanation: You don't have to repeat any other part of the transmission. It's all advisory information. You do not even have to repeat the frequency, but it is a good practice to do so. ATC will be able to correct your readback if you state the frequency incorrectly.

2. You make the frequency switch to Seattle Center on 133.4. Write the radio call you would make to the new controller:

_____

_____

↓↓ANSWER↓↓

"Seattle Center, Beechcraft 479TG, eight thousand fife hundred." (AIM 5-3-1 6. 2a. ATC Frequency Change Procedures.)

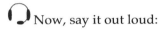 Now, say it out loud:

Explanation: First, since you are speaking to a new controller, you should resume using your full call sign. Second, with a positive radar handoff from the previous controller, the new controller will know your position over the ground and that you are VFR. All you need to verify with the new controller is your current altitude.

3. Continuing your flight in northern Washington State, you are approaching your destination of Bellingham, Washington. You want to end flight following service prior to contacting Bellingham Tower.

Write the radio call you would make to Seattle Center:

_____

_____

↓↓**ANSWER** ↓↓

"Beech 479TG would like to terminate flight following (or, terminate radar service.)" (AIM 4-1-5 b. 2. Radar Traffic Information Service.)

🎧 Now, say it out loud:

Switchology and Switch Timing

In this section, we are going to practice setting the switches of your aircraft radio correctly. Setting switches seems pilot-simple but pilots often get it wrong. Even highly experienced pilots occasionally mess up the switch settings on their radios. The result of incorrect switch usage can be anything from transmitting on the wrong frequency to interrupting an ongoing conversation on the radio.

The solution to incorrect switch setting is also pilot-simple. It involves something that is near and dear to your heart: checklists. In this case, I'm talking about a mental checklist, or habit pattern that you can repeat reliably each time you change the radio setup in the cockpit.

Define the following:

1. What does the transfer switch on your communication radio do?

_____

_____

↓↓**ANSWER** ↓↓

It transfers the frequency tuned into the standby window of your radio over to the active window of the radio. It also transfers the active frequency over to the standby window.

2. When a pilot says "Blocked" on the radio, what does he mean?

_____

_____

↓↓ANSWER↓↓

It means one person's transmission blocked or canceled out the transmission of someone else. (AIM Pilot/Controller Glossary.)

3. What should you do if you transmit a readback of a clearance given to you by ATC, and someone else says "Blocked" on the radio?

_____

_____

↓↓ANSWER↓↓

You should immediately repeat your readback of ATC's clearance. (AIM 4-2-2 Radio Technique.)

4. What should you do if you make a radio call, but you were not responding to an ATC clearance, and someone else says "Blocked" on the radio? For example, you are trying to check in on a new frequency and someone else says "Blocked" as soon as you stop transmitting.

_____

_____

↓↓ANSWER↓↓

You should pause long enough to let the other person, whom you blocked, repeat his last transmission. (AIM 4-2-2 Radio Technique.)

5. What could happen if a pilot pushes the transfer switch on his radio control head and then immediately starts transmitting on the new radio frequency?

_____

_____

↓↓ANSWER↓↓

That pilot stands a good chance of blocking someone else's transmission. (AIM 4-2-2 Radio Technique.)

Note: See the next question to deduce why immediately transmitting after switching frequencies might block some else's transmission.

6. Describe a technique that reduces the chances you will block another pilot's transmission when you switch to a new radio frequency.

_____

_____

↓↓ANSWER↓↓

Listen to make sure there is no ongoing conversation on the frequency. (AIM 4-2-2 Radio Technique.)

Note: As a technique, waiting 3 to 4 seconds before transmitting after switching to a new frequency will help you determine whether or not there is a conversation already in progress on the frequency.

7. When you listen to an ongoing conversation between a pilot and ATC, how do you know when it is okay to press the push-to-talk switch and make your own transmission?

_____

_____

↓↓ANSWER↓↓

When one of the people in the conversation finishes a readback, or acknowledgement, of information.

Explanation: As a general rule, every radio call made that passes information must be confirmed with an acknowledgement or readback. Advisory information should be acknowledged by stating your call sign, and possibly the word, "Roger."

Example:

Advisory transmission: "Seattle Center, King Air 3ER, back on your frequency."

Acknowledgement of the advisory: "King Air 3ER, Seattle Center, roger."

There is a very good discussion of techniques for timing your transmissions in *Radio Mastery for VFR Pilots*, Chapter 8: Switchology.

8. The Aeronautical Information Manual says you should monitor the universal emergency frequency, 121.5, also known as Guard, in a secondary radio if that radio is not being used for another purpose. Describe two reasons why the AIM says monitoring Guard is a good practice:

1. _____

_____

2. _____

_____

↓↓ANSWER↓↓

To listen for signals from Emergency Locator Transmitters (ELT). (AIM 6-2-5 ELT.)

To listen for communication from intercepting fighter aircraft. (AIM 5-6-2 a. 3. Interception Procedures.)

Explanation for item 2: Although it is not specifically stated in the AIM, it is implied that any warnings to aircraft approaching restricted/prohibited airspace will be made on 121.5. These warnings will occur, repeatedly, before intercepting aircraft are involved.

Monitoring Guard is a good idea, but doing so can have unintended consequences. For example, incorrectly setting your radio panel's transmit and receive switches may cause you to accidentally transmit routine information on the Guard frequency.

9. To understand how a pilot may accidentally transmit on Guard, let's step through an example. Looking at the illustration below, which radio is this pilot currently using to talk to Miami Center on frequency 134.0?

Circle the correct answer:

    Comm Radio 1.   Comm Radio 2.

↓↓**ANSWER** ↓↓

    Comm Radio 1.

10. What frequency is the pilot monitoring in Comm Radio 2?

↓↓**ANSWER** ↓↓

    121.5

11. The pilot wants to leave Miami Center's frequency for 2 minutes to talk to flight service. Write the radio call he should make to Miami Center to request 2 minutes off Miami's frequency: (His call sign is Piper 7XB.)

_____

_____

↓↓ANSWER↓↓

"Piper 7XB would like to leave your frequency for 2 minutes."

Note: This procedure and its exact phrasing are not described in the AIM. Good sense dictates you advise the air traffic controller before leaving the frequency, along with an expected time to return to the frequency. The closest the AIM comes to providing guidance in this situation is: "If you have been receiving services; e.g., VFR traffic advisories and you are leaving the area or changing frequencies, advise the ATC facility and terminate contact." (AIM 4-2-3 c. Contact Procedures.)

Now, say it out loud:

12. Miami Center says, "Piper 7XB, frequency change approved. Report back in 2 minutes." Still referring to the illustration above, describe what the pilot has to do to talk to Flight Service, on frequency 122.1 on Comm Radio number 2, but still monitor Miami Center on Comm Radio 1:

_____

_____

_____

↓↓ANSWER↓↓

He would tune 122.1 in the standby window of Comm Radio 2. He would press the transfer switch of Comm Radio 2 to move 122.1 into the active window. He would then rotate his transmit switch to Comm Radio 2. He would leave the listen switch for Comm Radio 1 in the on position.

Note: See the illustration below for the results of this pilot's actions.

13. The pilot finishes talking to Fight Service right at the 2-minute limit allowed by Miami Center. He hears another pilot start talking to Flight Service on 122.1 and he wants to get off the frequency ASAP. He thinks the quickest way to do this is to return Comm Radio 2 to 121.5. How could he accomplish this quickly?

_____

_____

↓↓ANSWER↓↓

He could press the transfer switch on Comm Radio 2, which would cause 121.5 to move from the standby window to the active window.

14. Just as the pilot accomplishes this step, he hears Miami Center calling him: "Piper 7XB, are you back on frequency?"

Which switch is currently activated that allows the pilot to hear Miami Center calling him?

_____

↓↓ANSWER↓↓

The listen switch for Comm Radio 1.

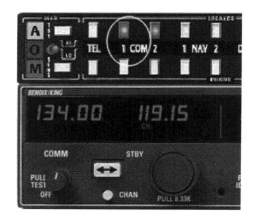

15. The pilot hits his push-to-talk switch says, "Miami Center, Piper 7XB is back on your frequency." Would Miami Center hear this transmission from the pilot?

Circle the correct answer:

    Yes. No. Maybe.

↓↓ANSWER↓↓

No.

16. Thinking back to what the pilot has done to the radio switches up to this point, in which position is the pilot's radio transmit selector?

Circle the correct answer:

    Comm Radio 1.   Comm Radio 2.

↓↓ANSWER↓↓

Comm Radio 2.

17. What frequency is the pilot currently transmitting on?

_____.

↓↓**ANSWER** ↓↓

121.5

18. What factor or factors caused the pilot to transmit on the wrong frequency?

_____

_____

↓↓**ANSWER** ↓↓

Rushing through the changes to the radio setup to meet the self-imposed 2-minute time limit to return to Miami Center's frequency; plus distraction by the radio transmission from the next pilot to use 122.1; and, the need to respond to the radio call from Miami Center.

There is a complete discussion of this exact scenario--its causes and solution, in *Radio Mastery for VFR Pilots*, Chapter 8, p. 134.

19. Rushing and distraction are 2 causes of errors in radio changes. A mental checklist or habit pattern will help you avoid errors. Devise a mental checklist for ensuring you don't make the same mistake. Write down the steps you would take after concluding a conversation on the Number 2 Comm radio. Adjust your radio

setup to make all subsequent transmissions on the Number 1 Comm radio while monitoring Guard on the Number 2 Comm radio:

1. _____

2. _____

3. _____

4. _____

5. _____

--Checklist Complete--

↓↓ANSWER↓↓

1. I will not rush. I will be deliberate in this process.

2. The frequency I want to use for Comm Radio 1 is in the active window for Comm 1.

3. The frequency I want to use for Comm Radio 2 is in the active window for Comm 2.

4. The transmit switch is positioned for the comm radio I want to use for talking.

5. The listen switches are positioned for the comm radios I want to monitor.

-Checklist Complete-

Note: The checklist you created does not have to match this one exactly. If your checklist helps you ensure you transmit and listen on the correct frequencies for your situation, your checklist is correct.

Communicating with Flight Service

If you have done any cross-country flying, you know how a Flight Service Station can support you before, during, and even after your flight. In this section, we will explore how to work with a FSS agent while you are in flight.

1. What are some of the reasons you might wish to contact a FSS while flying enroute?

1. _____

2. _____

3. _____

4. _____

↓↓ANSWER↓↓

The following is a complete list. You should be able to describe 4 of these reasons:

1. Activate or modify a flight plan.

2. Close a flight plan.

3. Update your progress on a flight plan by making a position report.

4. Get an update on weather and NOTAMs at your destination.

5. Get an update on weather along your route of flight.

6. Get help when you have become lost.

7. Ask for the applicable ATC frequency for your location.

8. General information, such as customs and immigration rules, Air Defense Identification Zone (ADIZ) rules and procedures, status of NAVAIDs, etc.

(Reference: Various locations in the AIM. FSS services related to weather is in AIM Chapter 7. Section 1. Meteorology.)

2. You have just departed the Greenwood County Airport in South Carolina. Your call sign is Cessna 437RW. Your destination is Williams Airport in Chapel Hill, North Carolina. You would like to activate your flight plan with flight service. Referring to the sectional chart below, what frequency should you dial into your comm radio to transmit to Flight Service?

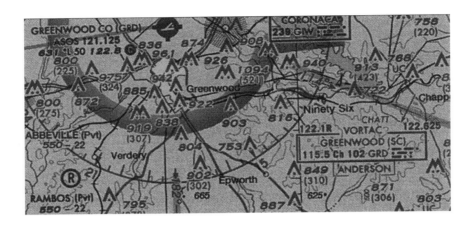

↓↓ANSWER↓↓

122.1 or 122.625 (Any Sectional Chart legend. *Radio Mastery for VFR Pilots*, Chapter 15, p. 266.)

Explanation: In the frequency listing above the box for the Greenwood VOR, you see 122.1R and 122.625. The "R" in 122.1R means the FSS receives transmissions on that frequency, but they do not transmit on that frequency.

4. What is the identifying name of the FSS you will be contacting?

↓↓ANSWER↓↓

Anderson Radio. (Any Sectional Chart legend. *Radio Mastery for VFR Pilots*, Chapter 15, p. 266.)

Explanation: The name Anderson is portrayed on the chart in brackets below the VORTAC information box. The word "Radio" is added to the call sign for all Flight Service Stations.

5. If you used 122.1 to transmit to the FSS, what frequency would you use to listen to replies from the FSS?

↓↓ANSWER↓↓

115.5. (Any Sectional Chart legend. *Radio Mastery for VFR Pilots*, Chapter 15, p. 266.)

Explanation: You would tune the VOR frequency 115.5 into a navigation radio and then adjust your radio control switch so you could listen to transmissions on the VOR frequency. You will hear the identifier for the VOR and voice transmissions from the FSS. Some aircraft radios have the capability to switch off the identifier transmissions from a VOR and listen to voice only.

6. If your communication radio does not tune frequencies out to the third decimal place (e.g. .000), could you still use the alternate frequency, 122.625, for this FSS?

Circle the correct answer:

   Yes. No. Maybe.

↓↓ANSWER↓↓

Yes.

Explanation: All VHF communication radios tune frequencies out to the third decimal place when tuning any frequency that has a 2 or a 7 in the second decimal place. For example, if your radio shows 122.62, it actually is tuning 122.625. A radio tuned to 133.47, for example, is actually tuned to 133.475. Since most air traffic controllers assign frequencies only to the second decimal place, most radio manufacturers build radios that do not show the third decimal place in their radios' frequency displays.

7. Trivia question: When you contact the FSS using the identifying name you wrote in the blank above, is the person you are speaking to at the FSS located in a facility in the town named above?

Circle the correct answer:

   Yes. No. Maybe.

↓↓ANSWER↓↓

Maybe.

Explanation: If you happen to be flying near the same location as an FSS hub or satellite facility, then coincidentally you'll be talking to a local person. Otherwise, it is likely you are talking to a person hundreds of miles away via a remotely located radio station.

8. Write the radio call you would make to establish contact on 122.1 with an agent at the FSS identifier you entered above: (Your call sign is Cessna 437RW.)

_____

_____

↓↓ANSWER↓↓

"Anderson Radio, Cessna 437RW receiving on the Greenwood VOR (or, receiving on 115.0)." (AIM 4-2-3 b. Initial Contact When Your Transmitting and Receiving Frequencies are Different.)

🎧 Now, say it out loud:

Explanation: When contacting an FSS, you need to tell the agent which frequency you are using <u>to listen</u> to his transmissions. FSS agents work with multiple frequencies in multiple locations. By telling the agent which frequency you are listening to, he will know which frequency to select to talk to you. In this case you are listening on the Greenwood VOR frequency, 115.5.

9. The agent says, "Cessna 437RW, this is Anderson Radio. Go ahead." Write your radio call to activate your flight plan. As a reminder, you are enroute to the Williams Airport (IGX) at Chapel Hill, North Carolina. You are currently 15 miles northwest of the Greenwood County Airport:

_____

_____

↓↓ANSWER↓↓

"Cessna 437RW is airborne, off of Greenwood County. I'd like to activate my flight plan to India Golf Xray. Over." (AIM 5-1-4 Flight Plan—VFR Flights.)

🎧 Now, say it out loud:

The agent says, "Cessna 437RW, Anderson radio copies. We'll activate your flight plan at 1735Z. After landing, you may close your flight plan with Raleigh Flight Service on 122.2 or 122.65. Is there anything else I can help you with today? Over." You tell the agent you do not need anything else. The agent replies, "Cessna 437RW, Anderson Radio copies. I'm clear at 1736Z."

10. Same day, same airplane, same flight plan. You are now 1 hour into your flight and you are approaching the Sandhills VORTAC. You would like to check in with Flight Service and provide a position report. Referring to the sectional chart below, what is the identifying name of the FSS you should call?

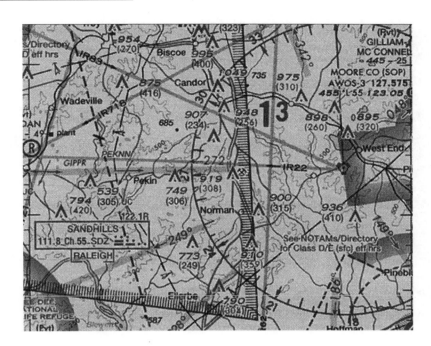

↓↓**ANSWER**↓↓

Raleigh Radio.

11. What frequency will you tune to <u>listen</u> to transmissions from the FSS?

_____.

↓↓**ANSWER**↓↓

111.8

12. What radio will you use to tune in the listening frequency?

_____.

Tune the listening frequency on a VOR navigation radio.

13. Write the radio call you would make to this FSS to establish contact:

_____

_____

↓↓**ANSWER** ↓↓

"Raleigh Radio, Cessna 437RW, receiving Sandhills VOR (or, receiving on 111.8)."

🎧 Now, say it out loud:

14. The agent at the FSS says, "Cessna 437RW, Raleigh Radio. Go ahead." Write your radio call to tell the FSS agent you intend to make a position report.

_____

_____

↓↓**ANSWER** ↓↓

"Cessna 437RW, with a position report. Are you ready to copy?"

🎧 Now, say it out loud:

Explanation: This courtesy call is a technique. You could launch right into your position report after making initial contact, but this courtesy radio call will help the agent prepare to copy your report.

15. The agent tells you he is ready to copy your report. You are currently 20 miles southwest of the Sandhills VORTAC, on the airway Victor 155. Your altitude is 5,500 feet MSL. Your new estimated time of arrival at the Williams Airport is 1845Z.

Write the radio call you would make to pass this information to the agent:

_____

_____

_____

"Cessna 437RW is 20 miles southwest of Sandhills on Victor one fife fife. Fife thousand, fife hundred feet. Estimated time of arrival at Williams is 1845 Zulu. Over." (AIM 5-1-4 g. Flight Plan—VFR Flights.)

Now, say it out loud:

16. The agent at the FSS repeats your position report word for word. Then the agent says, "Would you like the current and forecast weather for Williams Airport?" After stating your call sign, what is the single word you could say after your call sign to hear the current and forecast weather for Williams?

_____.

"Affirmative." (AIM Pilot/Controller Glossary.)

Note: The word "Roger" does not apply here. "Roger" means "message received."

17. The agent gives you his weather report and then asks if you would like the NOTAMs for the airport. Since you already have a complete list of NOTAMs for the airport, what is the single word you can use after your call sign that tells the agent you do not need to hear the NOTAMs?

_____.

"Negative." (AIM Pilot/Controller Glossary.)

18. The agent asks, "Cessna 437RW, do you have time to give an inflight report?" You do have the time. What information is the agent asking for?

1. _____

2. _____

3. _____

4. _____

5. _____

6. _____

↓↓**ANSWER**↓↓

The position report format: (AIM 7-1-20 Pilot Weather Reports PIREP.)

1. Sky conditions as observed from your cockpit, including clouds, precipitation, and visibility.

2. The current level of turbulence, or say "Smooth ride" if there is no turbulence.

3. Icing, if encountered.

4. The outside air temperature.

5. The measured or estimated wind direction and speed at your altitude. (Be sure to say your wind report is estimated if you do not have wind-measuring instrumentation on board, such as a GPS flight management system.)

6. Any other pertinent remarks.

Write an inflight report using any data you choose that covers the first 6 data points listed above. (Note: there is no answer key for this exercise.)

1.

2.

3.

4.

5.

19. You have landed at Williams Airport and have taxied clear of the active runway. You tune the first of the 2 frequencies the FSS agent told you use to close your flight plan with Raleigh Radio. After 3 attempts at contact, you receive no reply from Raleigh Radio. What should you do next?

_____

↓↓ANSWER↓↓

Try the second frequency given to you by the FSS agent. (AIM 5-1-14 Closing VFR/DVFR Flight Plans. CFR 91.153 b. VFR Flight Plan Cancellation.)

20. You try this, but you are still not able to make contact with Raleigh Radio. What should you try next?

_____

_____

↓↓ANSWER↓↓

Contact the FSS by cell phone or landline.

21. Let's back up and say you are able to make contact with Raleigh Radio on the first frequency you try. After establishing contact with the agent, write the radio you would make to close your flight plan:

_____

"Cessna 427RW is on the ground at Williams. Please close my flight plan."

🎧 Now, say it out loud:

Ground Operations at Tower-Controlled Airports

1. What is the difference between a movement area and a non-movement area?

_____

_____

A movement area is a part of an airport surface in which the movement of all vehicles, ground vehicles and aircraft, is controlled by ATC. Vehicular movement is not controlled in non-movement areas. (AIM Pilot/Controller Glossary.)

2. Trivia Question: At Class D airports, who controls the ground movement of aircraft crossing runways, the tower controller or the ground controller?

Circle the correct answer:

Ground. Tower. Control varies by airport.

Control varies by airport.

3. When is the Automatic Terminal Information Service (ATIS) recording normally updated?

_____

_____

_____

↓↓**ANSWER** ↓↓

ATIS is normally updated once per hour, usually between :50 past the last hour and the beginning of the next hour. (AIM 4-1-13 b.)

4. What would cause ATIS to be updated before its regularly schedule update time?

_____

_____

↓↓**ANSWER** ↓↓

When there is a significant change in weather conditions at the airport, or a notable change in some aspect of airport operations. (AIM 4-1-13 b.)

Explanation: A notable change may, for example, be the closure of a runway for some reason.

5. How can you tell ATIS has been updated since the last time you listened to it?

_____

↓↓**ANSWER** ↓↓

The ATIS identifier will change. (AIM 4-1-13 d.)

Explanation: If the last hour's ATIS identifier was Alpha, the next ATIS will carry the identifier Bravo.

6. When are you required to advise an air traffic controller that you have listened to the most current ATIS?

_____

When making initial contact with the first controller you speak to at that airport. (AIM 4-1-13 d.)

7. Let's say the most current ATIS is tagged with the identifier "Charlie." Write down the words you would say at the end of your initial contact with Ground Control that would indicate you have listened to the current ATIS:

_____

↓↓ANSWER↓↓

"With information Charlie." (AIM 4-1-13 d. Example.)

🎧 Now, say it out loud:

8. When a pilot contacts ATC and says, "With the numbers," does that mean he has listened to the current ATIS?

    Yes. No. (Circle the correct answer.)

↓↓ANSWER↓↓

No.

Explanation: "Use of this phrase means that the pilot has received wind, runway, and altimeter information ONLY and the tower does not have to repeat this information. It does not indicate receipt of the ATIS broadcast and should never be used for this purpose." (AIM 4-1-3 h. ATIS.)

9. You have called the ground controller for taxi instructions outbound to the runway and reported that you have listened to the most current ATIS. Assuming the ATIS does not change, when switching to the tower controller, are you required to report receiving the most current ATIS on initial contact with the tower controller?

Circle the correct answer:

    Yes. No. Maybe.

↓↓ANSWER↓↓

No. (AIM 4-1-13 d.)

10. Some airports have taxiway intersections that have been designated "Hot Spots". What is a Hot Spot?

_____

↓↓**ANSWER**↓↓

A Hot Spot is an intersection on the airport where there is a potential for aircraft to come into conflict with each other. (FAA Airport Facility/Directory, Airport Diagrams, Hot Spots.)

11. How is a Hot Spot depicted on an airport diagram?

_____

_____

↓↓**ANSWER**↓↓

A Hot Spot is depicted as an "HS" plus a number enclosed by a rectangular border. The type and rectangle are light brown in color. (FAA Airport Facility/Directory, Airport Diagrams, Hot Spots.)

Example: HS 1

12. What does a pilot have to do to commit a runway incursion?

_____

_____

↓↓**ANSWER**↓↓

A pilot would commit a runway incursion by crossing over any hold short line for that runway without authorization from the airport tower. (FAA Airport Facility/Directory, Airport Diagrams, Hot Spots.)

13. What are some techniques you can use to avoid committing a runway incursion?

1. _____

   _____

2. _____

   _____

3. _____

   _____

4. _____

   _____

↓↓ANSWER↓↓

Have the airport taxi diagram out and viewable before you begin taxiing.

Become an expert on the meaning of airport signs, lines and other markings.

Read back all runway hold short instructions to ATC.

State, out loud, to yourself, your intent to stop before crossing a hold short line if not cleared to cross the line.

If you are unsure whether you are authorized to cross or enter a runway, get clarification from ATC.

(FAA Airport Facility/Directory, Airport Diagrams, Hot Spots.)

When a ground controller issues taxi instructions, he will always begin by stating the runway identifier of the runway you will be using. For example, if an airport has 2 runways, Runway 30 and Runway 2, Ground might say, "Cessna 9130D, Runway 30." This means, of the 2 runways available, you will be taxiing to Runway 30 for departure.

Next, Ground Control will issue a taxi route that concludes at the place you are required to stop, or in taxi terms, "hold short." If Ground does not include the words "hold short," then the taxi route will take you all the way to the end of the runway where you are expected to hold short. A clearance all the way to a runway does not include a clearance to enter that runway.

14. When reading back your taxi clearance to Ground Control, you are required to include your call sign plus what three items of information?

1. _____

2. _____

3. _____

↓↓**ANSWER** ↓↓

"**(a)** The runway assignment.

(b) Any clearance to enter a specific runway.

(c) Any instruction to hold short of a specific runway or line up and wait."

(AIM 4-3-18 a. 9.)

15. If you are only required to read back the 3 items you listed above, why is reading back your entire taxi clearance a good practice?

_____

_____

↓↓**ANSWER** ↓↓

It allows the ground controller to listen to your readback and ensure you copied it correctly.

(*Radio Mastery for VFR Pilots*, Chapter 10, p. 163.)

16. You receive the following taxi clearance from Ground Control: "Cirrus 462AQ, Runway 30, taxi via Bravo. Hold short of Runway 27R." Write *only* the *required* readback items in this clearance.

1. _____ .

2. _____ .

3. _____ .

↓↓ANSWER↓↓

1. Cirrus 462AQ.

2. Runway 30.

3. Hold short of Runway 27R.

(AIM 4-3-18 a. 9.)

17. Write a full readback of the taxi clearance in exercise 16, including non-required items: (This is a best practice.)

_____

_____

↓↓ANSWER↓↓

"Cirrus 462AQ, Runway 30, taxi via Bravo. Hold short of Runway 27R."

At some airports, the only way to reach the end of the runway is by taxiing on the runway itself. Often, this means a pilot has to taxi on the runway in a direction that is opposite to the direction of takeoff.

For example, look at the airport diagram for Bowman Field (below). Runway 6 is depicted as 4,326 feet long. Notice that the taxiway that parallels Runway 6, Taxiway H, does not reach the end of Runway 6. Taxiway H terminates slightly past Taxiway G. This means the only way an airplane can use the full length of Runway 6 would be to enter the runway at Taxiway G and then taxi to the end of the runway.

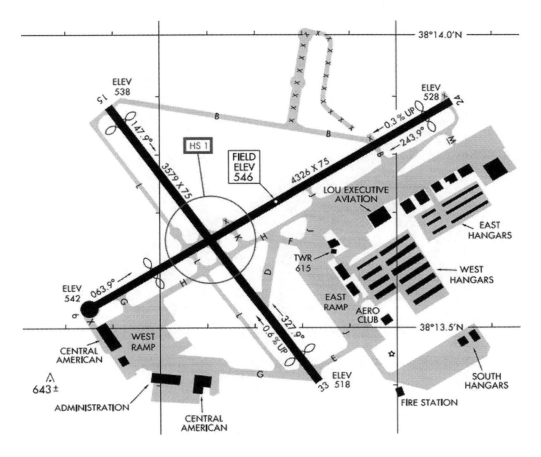

Runway 6 has a turnaround circle at its end to make it easier for a pilot to turn around for lineup after reaching the end of the runway. The process of taxiing on the runway, opposite the direction of takeoff, to reach the end of the runway is called "back taxiing." (In countries other than the U.S., this process is called "back tracking.")

The other option would be for Tower to direct you to begin your takeoff roll from abeam a taxiway intersection. In this case back taxiing is not authorized.

In my book *Radio Mastery for VFR Pilots*, I strongly recommend, as a technique, studying the airport diagram prior to calling Ground for taxi instructions. I also recommend, as a technique, that you mentally rehearse the various taxi routes from your parking position to the active runway(s). The point of mentally rehearsing taxi routes is to reduce the chance you will be surprised or confused by complex taxi instructions given to you by Ground. Let's practice some taxi briefings.

Here is an airport diagram for the Midland International Airport in Midland, Texas.

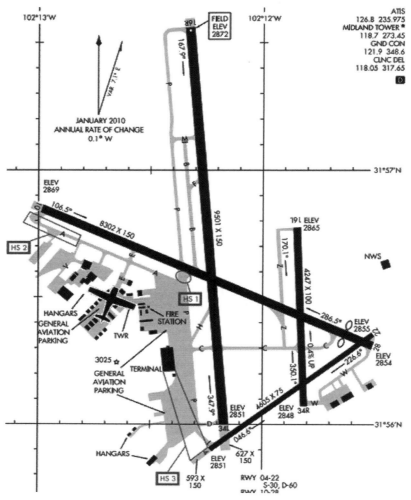

When you listen to the ATIS, you learn Tower is using Runway 34 Left (34L) for departures and landings. Runway 4 is also available, for departures only. Your airplane is parked on the ramp marked General Aviation Parking, near Taxiway E. Your aircraft's performance would allow a takeoff on either Runway 34L from the intersection at Taxiway C, or on Runway 4, full length. There are no NOTAMs affecting any taxiway or runway at this airport.

18. With this information in mind, write out the briefing for the taxi route you expect to receive from Ground Control that would get you from your parking position to the end of Runway 34L. Be sure to include any hold short instructions you might receive along the way:

_____

_____

↓↓ANSWER↓↓

Taxiway E to right on Alpha. Right on Papa. Left on Delta and hold short of Runway 34L.

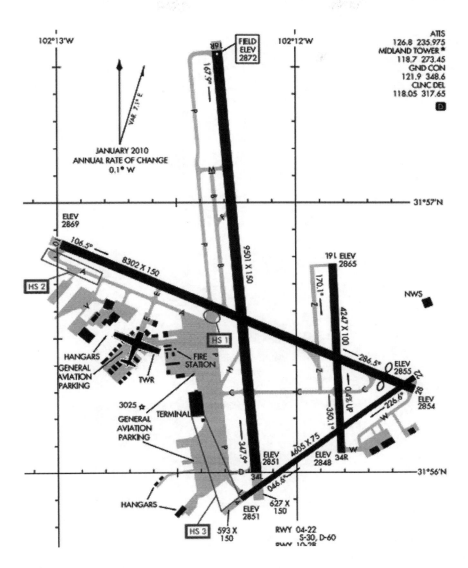

19. Now, write the anticipated taxi route to Runway 4 at Midland International:

_____

_____

_____

↓↓**ANSWER**↓↓

Taxiway E to right on Alpha. Right on Papa, then left on Lima to the end and hold short of Runway 4.

Here is an airport diagram for the Bob Hope Airport in Burbank, California.

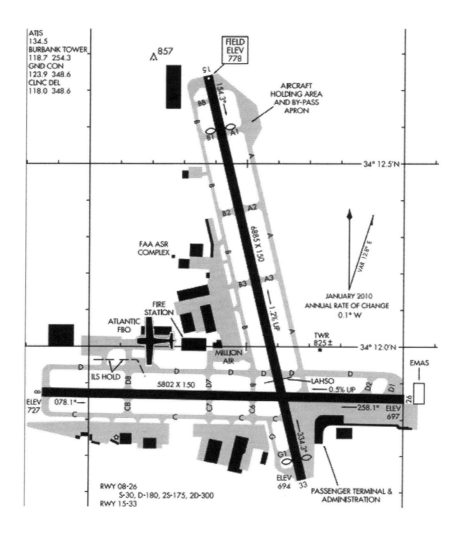

When you listen to the ATIS, you learn Tower is using Runway 33 for departures and landings. Your airplane is parked on the Atlantic FBO ramp, on the east side of Taxiway D8. There are NOTAMs for this airport that say Taxiway D7 is closed for construction.

20. With this information in mind, write out the briefing for the taxi route you expect to receive from Ground Control that would get you from your parking position to the end of Runway 33. Be sure to include any hold short instructions you might receive along the way:

_____

_____

_____

↓↓ANSWER↓↓

Exit parking with a left on Delta. Right on Bravo. Hold short of Runway 26. Then cross Runway 26 to join Charlie 6. Left Charlie. Right on Golf to the end and hold short of Runway 33.

Here is an airport diagram for the Dekalb-Peachtree Airport in Atlanta, Georgia.

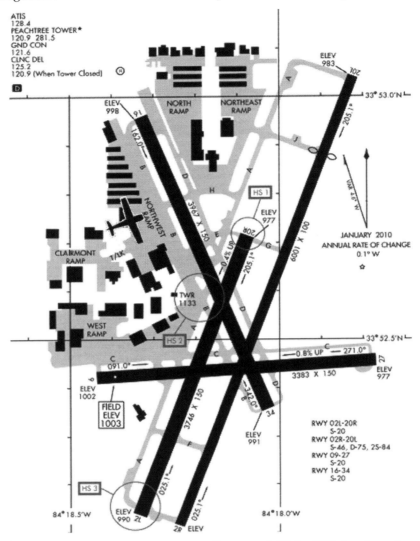

When you listen to the ATIS, you learn Tower is using Runway 2 Right (2R) for departures and landings. Runway 34 is also available for departures only. Your airplane is parked on the Northwest Ramp directly across from Taxiway H. Your aircraft's performance would allow a takeoff on either Runway 2R or on Runway 34. There are no NOTAMs affecting any taxiway or runway at this airport.

21. With this information in mind, write out the briefing for the most direct taxi route you expect to receive from Ground Control that would get you from your parking position to the end of Runway 2R. Be sure to include any hold short instructions you might receive along the way. (Correct answer is on the next page.):

_____

_____

_____

↓↓**ANSWER**↓↓

Right on Bravo. Right on Alpha. Hold short of Runway 9. Then cross Runway 9 on Alpha. Alpha to the end and hold short of Runway 2L. Then cross Runway 2L and hold short of Runway 2R.

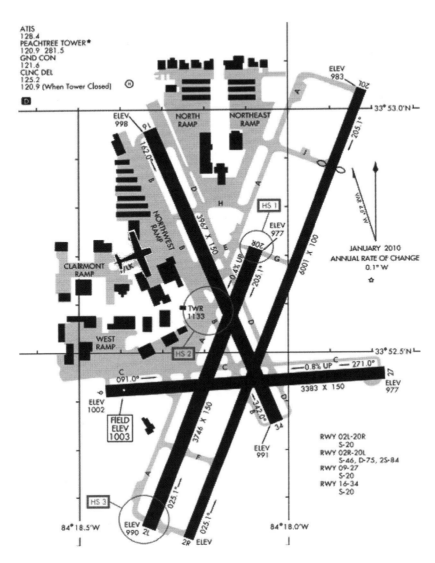

22. Now write the anticipated taxi route for Runway 34:

_____

_____

_____

_____

↓↓**ANSWER**↓↓

Right on Bravo. Hold short of Runway 2L. Then cross Runway 2L and continue on Bravo. Hold short of Runway 27. Then cross Runway 27 and continue on Bravo to the end. Hold short of Runway 34.

When receiving your taxi clearance from Ground, I recommend you:

1. Keep the airport diagram in front of you in a position where it is easily seen.

2. Write the taxi clearance on a piece of paper.

3. When writing the taxi clearance, use abbreviations rather than writing the clearance word for word.

For example, if Ground were to say, "Cessna 9130D, Runway 30. Taxi via left Alpha. Hold short of Runway 2," you could write:

    30 LA / 2

This interprets as Runway 30 (30), left Alpha (LA), hold short Runway 2 (/ 2).

Another example: "Cessna 9130D, Runway 16. Taxi via right Yankee, cross Runway 7, then left Hotel, right Papa. You could write:

    16 RY x7 LH RP

This can be read back as Runway 16 (16), via right Yankee (RY), cross Runway 7 (x7), left Hotel (LH), right Papa (RP). This is technique only. You can develop your own system.

The important point is to write only what you need to jog your memory. Do not write in complete sentences. Writing in complete sentences takes more time and concentration than you can afford. If you write a clearance in complete sentences, it's likely you will not be able to absorb every detail of Ground Control's clearance.

Let do a little more practice. Here are some example clearances.

23. In the space below each clearance, write your personal code that will help you remember the clearance:

"Cessna 9130D, Figmore Ground. Runway 8. Taxi via Alpha."

_____

↓↓ANSWER↓↓

8 A

🎧 Now, say it out loud:

24. "Cessna 9130D, Wiscasset Ground. Runway 24 Left. Taxi via left Charlie, right Delta 1, left Delta. Hold short of Runway 5 on Delta."

↓↓**ANSWER** ↓↓

24L LC RD1 LD/5

🎧 Now, say it out loud:

25. "Cessna 9130D, Alcott Ground, Runway 29. Taxi via Uniform. Cross Runway 1 Right. Hold short of Runway 1 Left."

↓↓**ANSWER** ↓↓

29 U X1R/1L

🎧 Now, say it out loud:

26. "Cessna 9130D, Bishop Ground, Runway 17. Taxi via right Charlie, left Delta. Hold short of Taxiway Foxtrot."

↓↓**ANSWER** ↓↓

17 RC LD/F

🎧 Now, say it out loud:

27. "Cessna 9130D, Executive Ground, Runway 33. Taxi via Alpha, then make the left turn onto Runway 20. Hold short of Taxiway Juliett on Runway 20."

↓↓**ANSWER** ↓↓

🎧 Now, say it out loud:

At some airports, the ground controller may use a runway as a taxiway. You are cleared to enter a runway and use it for taxiing only if the controller authorizes it for taxi. Runways may be used for taxiways at any time. You may expect them to be used for taxiing most often when they are not used for takeoff or landing.

After landing, you should not turn off of the landing runway onto another runway without authorization from Tower. As with taxiing out to a runway for takeoff, Tower may authorize the use of a runway as a taxiway after landing.

Using a runway as a taxiway also applies to the landing roll. After you have slowed to taxi speed, you are expected to exit the runway as directed or by using the next available taxiway to turn off of the runway. You may continue to roll on the runway after slowing to taxi speed, but you must get authorization from Tower to do so.

There is a more extensive discussion of taxi options in *Radio Mastery for VFR Pilots*.

Let's practice. Your call sign is Cessna 9130D. You have just landed on Runway 6, which is 8,000 feet long. After landing, you slow and reach taxi speed with 5,000 feet of runway remaining. Your parking spot is located near the end of Runway 6.

28. Write the radio call you would make to Tower to request continued taxi to the end of the runway:

_____

↓↓ANSWER↓↓

"Cessna 9130D request a roll to the end of the runway." (AIM 4-3-20 Exiting the Runway After Landing.)

🎧 Now, say it out loud:

Tower replies, "Cessna 9130D. Traffic is on a 7-mile final. You're cleared to expedite your taxi down Runway 6 and exit at Taxiway Hotel." Or, Tower may say, "Cessna 9130D, unable a roll to the end. Traffic is on a 3-mile final. Make the next left off the runway at Taxiway Lima." If Tower says "Unable" in response to your request, don't argue. Exit the runway as directed.

Speaking of speed permitting, never exit a runway after landing before you have decelerated to a safe taxi speed. I bring this up because sometimes a tower controller will ask you to exit the runway before you have reached a safe taxi speed. It is not that Tower wants you to taxi at an unsafe speed; Tower is striving to get you off the runway to make the runway available for other aircraft as quickly as possible.

29. When Tower says, "If able, make the next turn off the runway," is this a clearance or a request?

Circle the correct answer:

A clearance.   A request.

↓↓**ANSWER** ↓↓

A request.

Explanation: Tower is saying you should exit the runway only if you are down to a safe taxi speed. You are not required to exit the runway with this type of clearance.

30. If you cannot exit the runway this point because your groundspeed is too high, what should you say to Tower? Write your response below:

_____

_____

↓↓**ANSWER** ↓↓

"Cessna 9130D is unable the next turn off." Or, "Cessna 9130D cannot make the next turn." (AIM 4-3-20 Exiting the Runway After Landing.)

31. Tower says to you, "Cessna 9130D, make the next left at Taxiway Echo." Is this a clearance or a request?

Circle the correct answer:

A clearance.   A request.

↓↓**ANSWER** ↓↓

A clearance. (AIM 4-3-20 Exiting the Runway After Landing.)

Explanation: In this case, Tower is not giving you the option to bypass the next turn off the runway. You are legally required to comply with Tower's clearance unless you get an amended clearance. This does not mean you should make an unsafe exit off the runway.

32. Even though Tower has directed you to exit at the next taxiway, if your speed is not down to a safe taxi speed, what should you say to Tower?

_____

↓↓**ANSWER** ↓↓

"Cessna 9130D will be unable an exit at Echo." (AIM 5-5-2 a. 3. Air Traffic Clearance.)

33. Should you wait until you are passing Taxiway Echo at a high speed to make the statement above, or should you say the statement immediately in reply to Tower's direction?

Circle the correct answer below:

Wait until passing Echo.   Respond immediately.

↓↓**ANSWER** ↓↓

Respond immediately. (AIM 5-5-2 a. 4. Air Traffic Clearance.)

Explanation: Do not wait to get an amended clearance. Tower will assume you will make the turnoff if you do not reply that you are unable. By regulation, you must get an amended clearance from ATC before pursuing an alternate course of action. If you wait to get an amended clearance until you are passing the turnoff that Tower told you to use, you are actually violating an ATC clearance.

Tower should reply, in response to your statement that you will be unable the turnoff at Echo: "Cessna 9130D, speed permitting, exit the runway at . . . (the next taxiway after Echo)."

I also want you to realize, sometimes, Tower couldn't care less where and when you exit the runway. If the airport has little or no traffic other than your aircraft, Tower may not say anything about which taxiway to use to exit the runway. Alternately, the Tower controller may be too busy with other radio calls to address you as you roll out after landing. In either case, after slowing to a safe taxi speed, simply use the first available taxiway to exit the runway.

Tower may also say to you, "Any available right (or left) turn." This means, use your own discretion and exit when you are comfortable.

Let's practice a bit more. Your call sign remains Cessna 9130D. You have just landed on Runway 7. The next two available turnoffs from the runway are Taxiway B 1 and Taxiway B 2.

34. When Tower says, "Cessna 9130D, if able, make the next left turn off at Bravo 1." Your groundspeed is still too high to make a safe exit at B 1. Write your reply to Tower:

_____

↓↓**ANSWER** ↓↓

"Cessna 9130D is unable the turnoff at Bravo 1." (AIM 5-5-2 a. 3. Air Traffic Clearance.)

You have just landed on Runway 10. The next two available turnoffs from the runway are Taxiway C and Taxiway D.

35. When Tower says, "Cessna 9130D, traffic is 1 mile out for Runway 10. Make the next right turn at Charlie," your airspeed is still too high to make a safe exit at Taxiway Charlie. Write your reply to Tower:

_____

↓↓ANSWER↓↓

"Cessna 9130D is unable the turnoff at Charlie," Or, "Cessna 9130D can make the turnoff at Delta." (AIM 5-5-2 a. 1. Air Traffic Clearance.)

36. Reset the scenario but use the same setup. Runway 10, exits at Taxiways C and D, groundspeed too high to safely turnoff at Taxiway C. Tower says, "Cessna 9130D, are you able the next right turn at Charlie?" Write your reply to Tower:

_____

↓↓ANSWER↓↓

"Cessna 9130D, negative. We can make the turn off at Delta." (AIM 5-5-2 a. 3. Air Traffic Clearance.)

When exiting the runway, Tower may direct you to use a high-speed turnoff. A high-speed turnoff is a taxiway constructed at an angle to the runway that is less than 90 degrees relative to the runway's centerline. (See illustration, next page.)

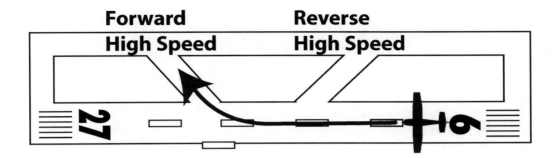

High Speed Turnoff Taxiways

The other high-speed turnoff, oriented to allow a quick exit from Runway 27, is called a "reverse high-speed" when landing on Runway 9.

While you are always welcome to use a forward high-speed turnoff, you must get authorization from Tower before using the reverse high-speed.

Why? Using a reverse high-speed involves reversing direction on the runway. The AIM says: "At airports with an operating control tower, pilots should not stop or reverse course on the runway without first obtaining ATC approval." (AIM 4-3-20 a.)

37. Write the radio call you would make to get Tower's permission to use the reverse high-speed turnoff to exit the runway:

_____

↓↓ANSWER↓↓

"Cessna 9130D would like to use the reverse high-speed." Or, "Cessna 9130D requests the reverse high-speed."

Procedures and Techniques for Taking Off from a Tower-Controlled Airport

Let's talk about what to do after you have taxied out to a runway in preparation for takeoff.

1. First, how do you know when it is appropriate to switch frequencies from Ground to Tower?

_____

↓↓ANSWER↓↓

It depends on the airport's local procedures.

Explanation: The answer is not always clear because it depends on the local procedures at the airport. If the local procedures are not clear, then it's best to follow the guidance in the Aeronautical Information Manual.

2. What is the AIM's guidance on when to switch frequencies from Ground Control to Tower?

_____

_____

_____

↓↓ANSWER↓↓

"Pilots of departing aircraft should communicate with the control tower on the appropriate ground control/clearance delivery frequency prior to starting engines to receive engine start time, taxi and/or clearance information. Unless otherwise advised by the tower, remain on that frequency during taxiing and runup, then change to local control frequency when ready to request takeoff clearance.

NOTE–

Pilots are encouraged to monitor the local tower frequency as soon as practical consistent with other ATC requirements." (AIM 4-3-14 a. Communications.)

At some airports, the ground controller will tell you when to switch to Tower. At other airports, there might be a sign near the edge of the taxiway that marks the point where you should switch to Tower frequency. The sign will say something to the effect of: "Aircraft monitor Tower 118.5 past this point."

The phraseology in that sign brings up an important point. In some situations, the ground controller will tell you to monitor the tower frequency. In other cases, the ground controller will tell you to contact the tower.

3. What is the difference between monitoring Tower and contacting Tower?

_____

_____

_____

↓↓ANSWER↓↓

"Monitor" means switch to Tower's frequency but don't say anything. Wait for the tower controller to contact you. "Contact" means switch frequencies and call the tower controller when you are ready for takeoff. (AIM Pilot/Controller Glossary.)

A strong word of warning: Never, never, never use the word "takeoff" unless you are responding to Tower's clearance to take off. Don't say, for example, "Cessna 9130D, ready for takeoff," or, "Cessna 9130D is not ready for takeoff." The word 'takeoff' can be as dangerous a loaded gun when handled incorrectly.

4. Why is using the word "takeoff" before actually being cleared for takeoff so dangerous?

_____

_____

_____

↓↓ANSWER↓↓

Using the word "takeoff" before being cleared to takeoff can result in misunderstanding that leads to a runway incursion.

Note: Strangely, the FAA prohibits air traffic controllers from using the word "takeoff" until actually clearing an airplane for takeoff. The FAA places no such restriction on pilots.

For an extensive discussion of runway incursions and the hazards of using the word "takeoff" at the wrong time, see *Radio Mastery for VFR Pilots*, p. 164.

5. With all of this in mind, write the radio call you would make to County Tower, after performing your pre-takeoff checks, that indicates you are ready to use Runway 30 for departure. (Your call sign is Cessna 9130D, and this will be your first contact with County Tower.)

_____

↓↓ANSWER↓↓

"County Tower, Cessna 9130 Delta is ready." Or, "County Tower, Cessna 9130 Delta, holding short of Runway 30."

Note: These are techniques designed for safety. They are not contained in the AIM.

6. County Tower will answer your radio call with one of 3 responses. What are they?

1. _____ .

2. _____ .

3. _____ .

↓↓ANSWER↓↓

"Cessna 9130D, hold short." (AIM Pilot/Controller Glossary.)

"Cessna 9130D, Runway 30, line up and wait." (AIM 5-2-4 Line Up and Wait.)

"Cessna 9130D, Runway 30, cleared for takeoff." (AIM Pilot/Controller Glossary.)

Explanation: Clearance 1 seems redundant. Obviously, you were holding short of the runway before Tower made this radio call to you. Why say the obvious? Tower has to say something in response to your ready call. To avoid any confusion, he will simply say, "Hold short." Any other type of response, such as "Roger," might be perceived as a clearance to do something other than hold short, so Tower sticks with the one and only phrase that does the job of ensuring you do not move: "Hold short."

7. Let's practice. Tower says to you, "Cessna 9130D, Runway Two Six Right, line up and wait. Traffic will be departing off the parallel runway." Write your reply to Tower:

_____

↓↓ANSWER↓↓

"Cessna 9130D, Runway Two Six Right, line up and wait." (AIM 5-2-4 Line Up and Wait.)

🎧 Now, say it out loud:

Explanation: You read back the clearance. You do not read back the advisory about traffic.

8. Tower says to you, "Cessna 9130D, the wind is two seven zero at one zero, Runway Two Six Right, cleared for takeoff." Write your reply to Tower:

_____

↓↓**ANSWER**↓↓

"Cessna 9130D, Runway Two Six Right, cleared for takeoff." (AIM Pilot/Controller Glossary.)

🎧 Now, say it out loud:

Often, Tower's takeoff clearance contains more information than a simple clearance to take off. Tower may give you post-takeoff instructions before clearing you for takeoff. These instructions will depend on your flight plan. If you wish to depart the airport traffic pattern with plans to travel elsewhere, Tower may give you a heading to fly after takeoff. If your plan is to remain in the airport pattern for landing practice, Tower will give you post-takeoff instructions about what to do to remain in the pattern.

There will be occasions when you want to depart from the airport and go elsewhere. Tower has 3 post-takeoff options for you. He can direct you to:

1. Fly a specific heading after takeoff. This may also be "Fly runway heading."

2. Depart "straight out."

3. Fly a general direction after takeoff.

4. Depart from a leg of the published traffic pattern.

9. If Tower tells you to fly runway heading, where can you find the specific runway heading Tower wants you to fly?

_____

↓↓**ANSWER**↓↓

On the airport's taxi diagram; or, in the listing for the airport in the Airport Facility/Directory.

10. Given that the lateral dimensions of Class D airspace are tailored to each tower-controlled airport, when outbound from an airport, how can you tell when you have exited the Class D airspace?

_____

_____

_____

↓↓ANSWER↓↓

By looking at the depiction of the Class D perimeter for the airport on a sectional chart.

Let's take all this information about departing an airport and roll it into some practice radio work. In all cases, your call sign will be Piper 3054V, doing your engine run-up while on Ground Control's frequency. (Didn't see that coming, did you?) In all cases, you will be departing the airport for a destination elsewhere.

11. Ground says, "Piper 3054V, when ready, monitor Tower 119.0." Write your reply to Ground:

_____

↓↓ANSWER↓↓

"Piper 3054V." Or, "Piper 3054V, will monitor Tower 119.0." Or, "Piper 3054V, 119.0."

◯ Now, say it out loud:

12. "Piper 3054V, Kelsey Tower, Runway One Eight, line up and wait. Traffic crossing down field." Write your reply to Tower:

_____

↓↓ANSWER↓↓

"Piper 3054V, Runway One Eight, line up and wait."

◯ Now, say it out loud:

Explanation: The part of the radio transmission in which Tower tells you traffic crossing down field is advisory only and does not need to be repeated.

13. "Piper 3054V, after departure, fly runway heading. Runway One Eight, cleared for takeoff." Write your reply to Tower:

_____

↓↓ANSWER↓↓

"Piper 3054V, fly runway heading, Runway One Eight, cleared for takeoff."

🎧 Now, say it out loud:

14. "Piper 3054V, traffic is a Cessna 172, slightly above you at your 11 o'clock and 2 miles. Report that traffic in sight." Write your reply to Tower assuming you see the Cessna:

_____

↓↓ANSWER↓↓

"Piper 3054V, traffic in sight." (AIM Pilot/Controller Glossary.)

🎧 Now, say it out loud:

15. "Piper 3054V, maintain visual separation from the Cessna and left turnout approved. Remain my frequency for further traffic advisories." Write your reply to Tower:

_____

↓↓ANSWER↓↓

"Piper 3054V will maintain visual separation from the Cessna. Left turnout approved. We'll remain your frequency."

🎧 Now, say it out loud:

16. When you are about 5 miles east of the airport, Tower says, "Piper 3054V, no observed or reported traffic in your vicinity. Frequency change approved." Write your reply to Tower:

_____

↓↓ANSWER↓↓

"Piper 3054V." Or, "Piper 3054V, switching."

🎧 Now, say it out loud:

Explanation: "Switching" is pilot shorthand for "I'm leaving your frequency."

17. If you are departing a tower-controlled airport VFR and the tower controller does not tell you to remain his frequency after takeoff, when may you leave the tower's frequency after takeoff?

_____

↓↓ANSWER↓↓

You may leave the tower's frequency any time after takeoff.

Explanation: The AIM does not contain any requirement or restriction on when you may change frequencies after takeoff from a tower-controlled airport. As a technique, if you do not have a pressing need to change to another frequency, you may consider monitoring the tower's frequency until exiting the airport's traffic area. Monitoring the tower's frequency while in the airport traffic area will help you stay aware of the traffic situation around you.

Good job. Let's put you back on the ground at the Easton/Newman Airfield (KESN) in Maryland. (See the airport diagram.)

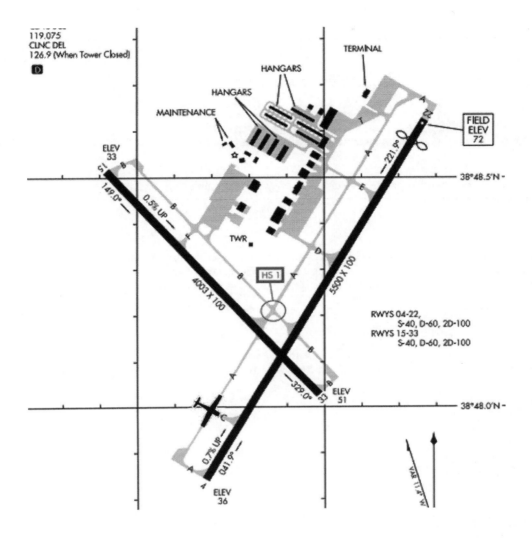

You are holding short of Runway 4 on Taxiway C, expecting an intersection departure. Your plan is to head southwest after takeoff to pick up routing to another airport. You have completed your pre-takeoff checklist and switched frequencies to Tower on 118.525 (118.52 in your radio's display window).

18. Write the radio call you would make to Easton Tower to indicate you are ready for takeoff, using the call sign Cirrus 715FD:

_____

↓↓ANSWER↓↓

"Easton Tower, Cirrus 715FD, ready at the intersection of Charlie and Runway 4." Or, "Easton Tower, Cirrus 715FD, holding short of Runway 4 at Charlie." (AIM 4-3-10 e. Intersection Takeoffs.)

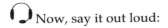 Now, say it out loud:

119

19. Tower says, "Cirrus 715FD, fly heading zero six zero, Runway 4 at Charlie, cleared for takeoff." Write your reply to Easton Tower:

_____

_____

↓↓ANSWER↓↓

"Cirrus 715FD, heading zero six zero, Runway 4 at Charlie, cleared for takeoff." (AIM 4-3-10 Intersection Takeoffs.)

🎧 Now, say it out loud:

Explanation: Remember, it's critical to include the named intersection from which you are cleared to take off. If you fail to include the named intersection, Tower will insist you say the intersection to ensure you do not intend to back taxi on the runway and use the runway's full length.

20. After takeoff, as you reach 1000 feet MSL, Easton Tower says, "Cirrus 715FD, right turnout to the southwest approved. Remain my frequency for traffic advisories." Write your reply to Easton Tower:

_____

_____

↓↓ANSWER↓↓

"Cirrus 715FD, right turnout to the southwest. We'll remain your frequency."

🎧 Now, say it out loud:

21. When Tower says, "Right turnout to the southwest approved," is there a specific heading you should fly? Circle the correct answer:

Yes. No. Maybe.

↓↓ANSWER↓↓

No.

Explanation: If Tower wanted you to fly a specific heading, he would say a specific heading. As long as you are flying some heading generally southwest, you are complying with Tower's instructions.

22. As you fly southwest, do you have to fly a specific track over the ground, such as the downwind leg of the airport traffic pattern, until you exit the airport traffic area?

Circle the correct answer:

　　Yes.　No.　Maybe.

↓↓ANSWER↓↓

　　No. (A complete discussion of headings to fly after takeoff can be found in *Radio Mastery for VFR Pilots*, p. 253.)

Easton Tower says, "Cirrus 715FD, traffic is a Beech Baron at your 1 to 2 o'clock and 3 miles. Do you have that traffic in sight?" You check 1 to 2 o'clock and see a twin-engine aircraft slightly above your altitude. It appears the aircraft will pass your off your right side with plenty of spacing.

23. Write your radio call to Easton Tower:

_____

↓↓ANSWER↓↓

　　"Cirrus 715FD, traffic in sight."

🎧 Now, say it out loud:

Easton Tower says, "Cirrus 715FD, roger. No other observed traffic in your vicinity. Frequency change approved."

24. Write your radio call to Easton Tower:

_____

_____

"Cirrus 715FD, switching."

🎧 Now, say it out loud:

Arriving at a Tower-Controlled Airport (Class D Airspace)

You are on your cross-country flight from Easton, Maryland to Charlottesville, Virginia. You are in contact with Washington Center for VFR flight following. About 25 miles northeast of the airport, you tune your secondary comm radio to ATIS:

"Charlottesville-Albemarle Airport information Tango, one eight fife fife Zulu weather. Four thousand scattered. Visibility seven. Temperature one fife. Dewpoint one zero. Wind two zero zero at one zero. Altimeter tree zero zero two. Runway Two One in use. Notices to Airmen, use caution for numerous birds in the vicinity of the airport. All aircraft contact Ground Control on 121.9 prior to taxi. Read back all runway hold short instructions. Advise on initial contact that you have received information Tango."

1. You are now 15 miles northeast of the airport and you are planning to contact Charlottesville Tower. Write the radio call you would make to Washington Center to end flight following prior to contacting Tower. (Your call sign is Cirrus 715FD.)

_____

_____

"Cirrus 715FD would like to terminate flight following (or, terminate radar service)." (AIM 4-2-3 c. Subsequent Contacts and Responses to Callup from a Ground Facility.)

🎧 Now, say it out loud:

2. When inbound to a Class D airport, when must you establish radio contact with the airport tower inside the Class D?

_____

You must be in contact with the airport tower prior to entering Class D. (AIM 3-2-5 b. 3. Class D Airspace.)

3. If you attempt to contact Tower and all you get in reply is "[your call sign], standby," does "Standby" constitute radio contact?

Circle the correct answer:

Yes. No. Maybe.

↓↓**ANSWER** ↓↓

Yes. (AIM 3-2-5 b. 3. Note 1. Class D Airspace.)

Explanation: The Aeronautical Information Manual says a response of "Standby" is considered radio contact.

4. What would Tower have to say to you to prevent you from entering his Class D airspace?

_____

↓↓**ANSWER** ↓↓

"Remain clear of (or, remain outside of) the Class D." (AIM 3-2-5 b. 3. Note 2. Class D Airspace.)

5. Fill in the blank: As a technique, it's a good idea to contact Tower about _____ miles from the airport's geographic center.

↓↓**ANSWER** ↓↓

10.

Explanation: This is technique only. Attempting contact 10 miles prior will give you adequate time to coordinate with Tower before entering his Class D airspace. You do not have to measure this distance precisely.

Some airports have charted landmarks that a pilot may use to report his position prior to entering the Class D. Charted landmarks are large, prominent features on the ground, easily recognizable from the air. They are tagged on terminal area charts with a magenta flag symbol. (See the example below.)

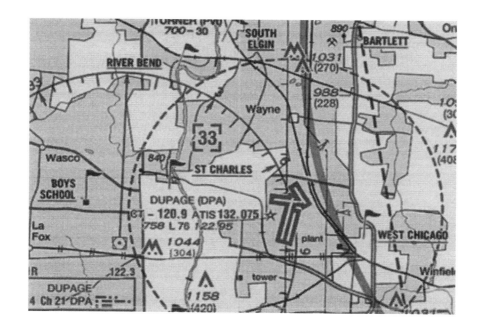

Magenta flags at River Bend, Boys School, West Chicago.

6. Are you required to fly over a charted landmark, if one exists, in order to enter an airport traffic pattern?

Circle the correct answer:

Yes. No. Maybe.

↓↓ANSWER↓↓

No.

Explanation: They simply exist for convenience. Tower controllers are familiar with these landmarks. Most pilots choose to overfly them when approaching airports where charted landmarks exist because they make position reporting easier. For example, "Dupage Tower, N468UP, over the river bend, inbound for landing."

7. You are flying Piper 263EZ on a cross-country over western Kansas. You are currently 15 miles east of the Garden City Airport (KGCK). The airport elevation is 2891 feet. What is the altitude, in mean sea level, of the top of Garden City Airport's Class D airspace, rounded up to the nearest 10 feet? (Assumes a standard Class D ceiling of 2,500 feet above airport elevation.)

_____ MSL

↓↓ANSWER↓↓

5,400.

Explanation: 2,891 + 2,500 = 5,391 or 5,400 when rounded up.

You would like pass through the airport's Class D airspace at 4,500 feet MSL as you proceed west. Your cruising altitude will place you inside the Class D as you fly over the airport.

8. What term do pilots and ATC use to describe passing through an airspace class?

_____.

↓↓ANSWER↓↓

Transition. (AIM Pilot/Controller Glossary.)

9. As you approach a point 10 miles east of the airport, you make your radio call to Garden City Tower to request permission to fly over the airport. Write the radio call you would make:

_____

_____

↓↓ANSWER↓↓

"Garden City Tower, Piper 263EZ, one zero miles east of the airport. Request a transition to the west at 4,500 feet."

🎧 Now, say it out loud:

Tower then approves your request to transition the airport. ATC says, "Piper 263EZ, report 5 miles west of the airport."

10. Several minutes pass and you are now at the reporting point requested by Tower. Write the radio call you would make to Tower:

_____

_____

↓↓ANSWER↓↓

"Piper 263EZ is 5 miles west of the airport."

Now, say it out loud:

Tower replies, "Piper 263EZ, roger. Frequency change approved." There are cases in which Tower will give you specific directions about how the controller wants you to overfly the airport. For example, "Piper 263EZ, cross over Runway One Eight at midfield." Or, "Piper 263EZ, remain north of the control tower as you transition the airport." There are many other variations. Listen up and read back Tower's instructions exactly as given.

New day, new airplane. You are now 10 miles northeast of the Charlottesville Airport, on Tower's frequency. Before you switched to Tower's frequency, you listened to the ATIS and noted the latest airport information was titled "Echo."

11. Write the radio call you would make to Charlottesville Tower, notifying the controller you are on your way in for touch-and-goes at the airport. (Your call sign is Cirrus 715FD.)

_____

_____

↓↓ANSWER↓↓

"Charlottesville Tower, Cirrus 715FD is 10 miles northeast of the airport, inbound for touch-and-goes, with information Echo."

Now, say it out loud:

Tower has several options when directing you to enter the airport traffic pattern. In each case, Tower will include the identifier for the runway he wants you to use:

1. Enter a midfield downwind.
2. Enter a base leg.
3. Enter a dogleg to final approach.
4. Enter a _____-mile straight-in approach.

Or, Tower may have you continue inbound and decide how to have you enter the pattern as you get closer. In this case, Tower says to you, "Cirrus 715FD, Charlottesville Tower, report 5 miles northeast."

12. Write your reply to Tower:

_____

_____

↓↓ANSWER↓↓

"Cirrus 715FD will report 5 miles northeast."

🎧 Now, say it out loud:

13. You are now 5 miles northeast of the airport. Write your radio call to Tower:

_____

_____

↓↓**ANSWER**↓↓

"Cirrus 715FD is 5 miles northeast."

🎧 Now, say it out loud:

14. Tower says to you, "Cirrus 715FD, report a left base for Runway Two One, and say your intentions after this touch-and go." Your intentions are to remain in the pattern for touch-and-goes. Write your reply to Tower:

_____

_____

↓↓**ANSWER**↓↓

"Cirrus 715FD will report a left base for Runway Two One. We would like multiple touch-and goes."

🎧 Now, say it out loud:

15. You are now on a left base for Runway 21. Write your radio call to Tower:

_____

↓↓**ANSWER** ↓↓

"Cirrus 715FD, left base, Runway Two One."

🎧 Now, say it out loud:

16. Tower says, "Cirrus 715FD, traffic is a Cessna 172 on departure roll. Runway Two One, cleared touch-and-go." Write your reply to Tower:

_____

↓↓**ANSWER** ↓↓

"Cirrus 715FD, Runway Two One, cleared touch-and-go."

🎧 Now, say it out loud:

17. You have completed your first touch-and-go. As you climb away from the runway, Tower says, "Cirrus 5FD, make right traffic. Report downwind." Write your reply to Tower:

_____

↓↓**ANSWER** ↓↓

"Cirrus 5FD, make right traffic. We'll report downwind."

Note: Tower switched to your abbreviated call sign, which means you can use your abbreviated call sign from this point forward. Do not forget to include your aircraft's make, model or type—Cirrus, in this case--when using your abbreviated call sign.

🎧 Now, say it out loud:

Some airports have a published traffic flow to the left or to the right for a particular runway. For example, a runway may have a left-hand traffic pattern only. At other airports, Tower may direct you to fly either a left-hand pattern or a right-hand pattern. If the airport pattern is not restricted to either direction, you may request to fly a particular pattern direction for each circuit around the pattern.

18. You are now on a right downwind for Runway 21. Write your radio call to Tower:

_____

↓↓ANSWER↓↓

"Cirrus 5FD, downwind."

🎧 Now, say it out loud:

Explanation: Note Tower did not tell you to report a right downwind. He simply said, "Report downwind."

19. Tower says, "Cirrus 715FD, Runway Two One, cleared touch-and-go,." Write your reply to Tower:

_____

↓↓ANSWER↓↓

"Cirrus 715FD, Runway Two One, cleared touch-and-go."

🎧 Now, say it out loud:

Note: This airport has more than 1 runway in use. That is why Tower says the runway's identifier with each clearance. You should also repeat the runway identifier in each readback. If the airport had only one runway, Tower would not state the runway identifier with each clearance.

20. You complete another touch-and-go. As you climb away from the runway, you decide you would like to make a left-hand circuit around the pattern. Write your radio call to Tower:

_____

↓↓ANSWER↓↓

"Cirrus 5FD, requests left traffic."

♪ Now, say it out loud:

21. Tower says, "Cirrus 5FD, left closed traffic approved. Report downwind." Write your radio call to Tower:

_____

_____

↓↓ANSWER↓↓

"Cirrus 5FD, left closed traffic. We'll report downwind."

♪ Now, say it out loud:

22. Notice Tower added one additional word in his last clearance that he did not say when he previously cleared you to make right traffic. He said, "Left closed traffic . . ." What does "closed traffic" mean?

_____

_____

↓↓ANSWER↓↓

"Closed traffic" means a pilot is authorized to make continuous circuits around the traffic pattern without further clearance from Tower. (AIM Pilot/Controller Glossary.)

Note: "Closed traffic approved" is not authorization to land after each circuit. Clearance to land must be obtained for each circuit. (AIM 4–3–2 b. Airports with an Operating Control Tower.)

23. If Tower does not specify a direction of turn, when he says, "Closed traffic approved," which direction are you authorized to turn on each circuit around the pattern? (There are traffic patterns available on both sides of the runway.)

_____

_____

↓↓ANSWER↓↓

"If not otherwise authorized or directed by the tower, pilots of fixed-wing aircraft approaching to land must circle the airport to the left." (AIM 4–3–2 b. Airports with an Operating Control Tower.)

24. As you reach downwind this time, you decide you would like to practice a go-around as you approach the runway threshold. Write your radio call to Tower to make this request for a low approach:

_____

_____

↓↓ANSWER↓↓

"Cirrus 5FD, requests a low approach."

🎧 Now, say it out loud:

25. Tower says, "Cirrus 5FD, I have your request. Continue on the downwind. I'll call your base." Write your reply to Tower:

_____

_____

↓↓ANSWER↓↓

"Cirrus 5FD will continue on the downwind."

Note: You may also add, "Call my base." However, replying "continue on the downwind" implies you will not turn off of downwind until Tower directs you to turn to base leg.

🎧 Now, say it out loud:

Immediately after you reply to Tower, you hear Tower say, "King Air 5526V, Runway 21, cleared for takeoff." The pilot of the King Air replies and you see the aircraft take the runway for departure. There are also 2 more aircraft waiting in line for the runway. Tower says, "Piper 405GG, Runway 21, line up and wait." The pilot of the Piper replies and you see his aircraft enter the runway.

When Tower has aircraft waiting to depart from the runway you are using, the controller may delay your turn towards the runway to gain time to launch those other aircraft. That is what is happening right now as Tower tells you to extend your downwind.

26. Tower says to you, "Cirrus 5FD, start your base turn now. Runway Two One, cleared low approach." Write your reply to Tower:

_____

_____

↓↓ANSWER↓↓

"Cirrus 5FD, turning base. Runway Two One, cleared low approach."

🎧 Now, say it out loud:

27. After your low approach, you climb out and make a left turn to the crosswind leg without hearing anything from Tower. Your closed traffic clearance is still in effect. As you reach downwind, Tower says, "Cirrus 5FD, Runway 21, cleared for the option." What does "cleared for the option" mean?

_____

_____

↓↓ANSWER↓↓

You are authorized to make a touch-and-go, a stop-and-go, a low approach, or a full stop landing at your discretion. (AIM Pilot/Controller Glossary.)

28. As you approach the turn to base leg, you hear another airplane report a 3-mile final approach for Runway 21. Tower clears that airplane to land, then says to you, "Cirrus 5FD, you are following a Piper Cub on a 3 mile final. Report that aircraft in sight." You see the Piper Cub, and you say:

_____

_____

↓↓ANSWER↓↓

"Cirrus 5FD, traffic in sight."

🎧 Now, say it out loud:

29. You continue your pattern. When you roll out on final approach, the Piper Cub is only a half-mile in front of you. The spacing between your aircraft and the Cub looks uncomfortably close. You would like to fly an S-turn maneuver to build a little more spacing behind the Cub. Write the radio call you would make to

Tower to advise him you would like to make S-turns:

_____

_____

↓↓**ANSWER** ↓↓

"Cirrus 5FD would like to S-turn for spacing."

🎧 Now, say it out loud:

Tower says, "Cirrus 5FD, approved as requested." You make your S-turns and the spacing behind the Cub improves.

There is a variation on this maneuver that may occur at an airport where aircraft are landing on parallel runways. If you request an S-turn maneuver, the controller may authorize the maneuver with the restriction to only turn away from the other parallel runway. Tower's intent when landing traffic on parallel runways is to avoid having you S-turn toward traffic on final approach for the other runway.

Let's return to your ongoing pattern work at Charlottesville Airport. As you complete your next touch-and-go, you hear another airplane check in on the frequency: "Charlottesville Tower, Cessna 325FD, 10 west of the airport. Inbound for landing." Tower says, "Cessna 325FD, report 5 miles west of the airport. Be advised there is a Cirrus 715FD also on this frequency. Use caution." The other pilot replies to this radio call. Then Tower says to you, "Cirrus 715FD, be advised there is a Cessna 325FD on the frequencies. Use caution."

30. Write your reply to Tower:

_____

_____

↓↓**ANSWER** ↓↓

"Cirrus 715FD." (AIM 4-2-4 a. 2. Aircraft Call Signs.)

🎧 Now, say it out loud:

Explanation: You only need to respond with your full call sign. Be sure to resume using your full call sign.

There is a complete discussion of the appropriate times to use your full call sign or your abbreviated call sign in *Radio Mastery for VFR Pilots*, Chapter 4.

As you complete your next touch-and-go, you hear, "Cessna 325FD, 5 west of the airport." Tower says, "Cessna 325FD, report a right base for Runway 21." The pilot of the Cessna replies to Tower.

31. You make left turns around the pattern as before. As you approach your turn for base leg, you hear, "Cessna 325FD, right base, Runway 21." Tower replies, "Cessna 325FD, roger. Break, break, Cirrus 715FD, make a right 360." Write your reply to Tower:

_____

_____

↓↓ANSWER↓↓

"Cirrus 715FD, making a right 360."

Now, say it out loud:

32. Why did Tower direct you to make a right-hand 360-degree turn?

_____

_____

↓↓ANSWER↓↓

To build spacing behind the other aircraft entering the traffic pattern from right base leg.

As you initiate your 360-turn, Tower says, "Cessna 325FD, cleared to land, Runway Two One. The wind is 190 at 15, gust 20." The pilot of the Cessna answers this clearance.

33. As you complete 3/4 of your circle, Tower says to you, "Cirrus 715FD, Runway Two One, cleared touch-and-go. Wind is 200 at 15, gust 25." You reply to Tower and continue to a base leg. As you roll out on final, you would like to check the winds again. Write your radio call to Tower to ask about the wind:

_____

↓↓ANSWER↓↓

"Wind check."

Explanation: This is one of very few radio calls in which you do not have to include your call sign. A wind check from Tower helps all pilots on the frequency, so Tower does not care who asked for it. By the way, "wind check" is not described anywhere the AIM. However, the Air Traffic Controller Manual J.O. 7110.65 requires controllers to provide wind information to pilots as needed.

PIREP

Tower says, "220 at 18, gust 27." On final approach, at 400 feet above the ground, your airspeed drops 20 knots almost instantly. You apply takeoff power and perform a windshear recovery maneuver.

1. After you recover the aircraft to stable flight, you are no longer in a safe position to land. Do you need authorization from Tower to perform a go-around before you can commence the go-around maneuver in this situation?

Circle the correct answer:

Yes. No. Maybe.

↓↓ANSWER↓↓

No.

Explanation: You absolutely <u>should not delay</u> a go-around for safety while trying to coordinate clearance from Tower. *After* you have safely begun a go-around, and feel comfortable taking on the additional task of making a radio, make an advisory call to Tower stating you are going around.

You execute your go-around and climb safely away from the runway. At this point, it would be helpful to let Tower know about the windshear. Your radio call advising Tower of the situation will allow the controller to warn other pilots about the danger.

When you want to make an advisory call to ATC warning of potentially unsafe flying conditions, you should use the acronym PIREP, meaning Pilot Report. Include the word "PIREP" in your radio call. For example, "Tower, Cirrus 715FD, PIREP. There's a large flock of birds 1/2 mile off the departure end of the runway at 500 feet, traveling south." Caution: Never make a PIREP in the middle of recovering to safe flight conditions. Wait until you have exited the hazardous situation and have returned to safe flight before making a PIREP. (AIM 7-1-20 Pilot Weather Reports PIREPs.)

2. Write your radio call to Tower, advising the controller of the windshear condition you encountered on final approach. Be as specific as possible in your description:

_____

_____

↓↓ANSWER↓↓

"Tower, Cirrus 715FD, PIREP. Loss of two zero knots at 400 feet on final."

( ) Now, say it out loud:

3. For the moment, let's remove you from the airport pattern at Charlottesville and place you in cruise flight over Maryland. You are in contact with Washington Center for flight following. Presently you are 30 miles southwest of the Hagerstown VOR at 5,500 feet MSL. The air is very turbulent.

Suddenly, you experience a 40-knot loss of airspeed as your airplane rolls abruptly to 60-degrees left bank. Your airplane loses 1,500 feet of altitude before you can recover to level flight and cruise airspeed. It's clear you have just encountered severe turbulence. Now that you are back in stable flight, make a PIREP to Washington Center about your encounter:

_____

_____

↓↓ANSWER↓↓

"Washington Center, Cirrus 715FD, PIREP. We hit severe turbulence at 5,500."

( ) Now, say it out loud:

Note: The controller may then ask you for additional detail. He may also ask if you require further assistance. He's questioning whether you think the turbulence might have damaged your aircraft. It's a good question.

4. That situation is over. Let's return you to present day and time, back in the airport pattern at Charlottesville. You are on downwind and you have decided it's time to get on the ground and park until the winds reduce in strength. Write your radio call to Tower announcing your decision to land:

_____

_____

↓↓ANSWER↓↓

"Cirrus 715FD would like to make this a full stop."

( ) Now, say it out loud:

5. Tower says, "Cirrus 715FD, Runway Two One, cleared to land. The wind is 200 at 18, gust 23." Write your reply to Tower:

_____

_____

↓↓**ANSWER**↓↓

"Cirrus 715FD, Runway Two One, cleared to land."

Now, say it out loud:

6. After you land and while still on landing roll, Tower says, "Cirrus 715FD, did you encounter any windshear that time?" Don't feel obligated to answer Tower until you have slowed to a safe taxi speed and have a taxiway turnoff in sight. You are now comfortably slowed to taxi speed. You don't recall encountering windshear on this approach. Write your radio call to Tower:

_____

_____

↓↓**ANSWER**↓↓

"Cirrus 715FD, did not encounter any windshear." Or, "Cirrus 715FD, negative windshear."

Now, say it out loud:

7. Tower replies, "Cirrus 715FD, roger. Any left turn off the runway." Write your reply to Tower:

_____

_____

↓↓**ANSWER**↓↓

"Cirrus 715FD, any left turn off the runway."

Now, say it out loud:

Note: If you have a taxiway targeted for your exit, you may tell Tower which taxiway you plan to use. Naming your taxiway is a courteous technique, but certainly not required.

8. The next taxiway turnoff is Taxiway C. As you exit at C, Tower says, "Cirrus 715FD, contact Ground, 121.9." Write your reply to Tower:

_____

_____

↓↓ANSWER↓↓

"Cirrus 715FD." Or, "Cirrus 715FD, point niner."

🎧 Now, say it out loud:

Note: As a reminder, when responding to a ground control frequency that begins with 121, you may skip saying 121 and only state the number to the right of decimal point, in this case, .9. (AIM 4-3-1 4. b. Communications.)

9. As you switch to Charlottesville Ground Control's frequency you see the FBO, Seventy-Five Cents Air, almost directly ahead. Taxiway C does not continue all the way to the parking area, but instead leads to the parallel Taxiway A. Write the radio call you would make to contact Ground:

_____

_____

↓↓ANSWER↓↓

"Charlottesville Ground, Cirrus 715FD, clear of the runway on Charlie. Going to Seventy-Fife Cents Air."

🎧 Now, say it out loud:

10. The ground controller says, "Cirrus 715FD, Charlottesville Ground, taxi to parking via right on Alpha and left on Foxtrot." Write your reply to Ground:

_____

_____

"Cirrus 715FD, right on Alpha, left on Foxtrot."

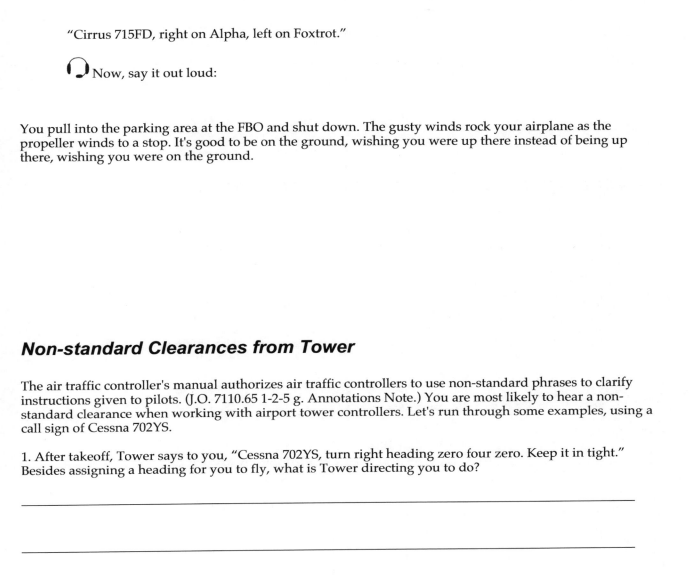 Now, say it out loud:

You pull into the parking area at the FBO and shut down. The gusty winds rock your airplane as the propeller winds to a stop. It's good to be on the ground, wishing you were up there instead of being up there, wishing you were on the ground.

Non-standard Clearances from Tower

The air traffic controller's manual authorizes air traffic controllers to use non-standard phrases to clarify instructions given to pilots. (J.O. 7110.65 1-2-5 g. Annotations Note.) You are most likely to hear a non-standard clearance when working with airport tower controllers. Let's run through some examples, using a call sign of Cessna 702YS.

1. After takeoff, Tower says to you, "Cessna 702YS, turn right heading zero four zero. Keep it in tight." Besides assigning a heading for you to fly, what is Tower directing you to do?

_____

_____

Tower wants you to make the tightest turn possible when you turn to zero four zero.

Note: This does not mean you should exceed 30 degrees of bank.

2. You are on base leg for a full stop landing. You see another airplane entering the runway for departure. Tower says to you, "Cessna 702YS, Runway 27, cleared to land. Square your base." What is Tower directing you to do and why?

_____

_____

_____

↓↓ANSWER↓↓

Fly a base leg until reaching a point where you can make one continuous, standard rate turn to final. This puts you on a longer final approach and gives Tower extra time to launch an airplane off your runway before you land.

Explanation: To understand why Tower would do this, you need to visualize the geometry of the traffic pattern created by a "square" turn from base to final. Many pilots initiate a turn to final approach early—cut the corner from base to final approach—which results in a short final approach leg. By requiring you to wait until the last possible moment to turn from base leg to final approach, Tower is forcing you to fly the longest final approach possible given where you started on base leg. A picture is worth a thousand words. See the illustration below to clarify this explanation.

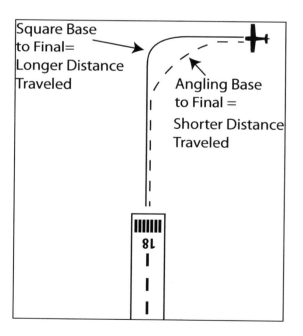

3. You have just reported 5 miles northeast of the airport. The landing runway is Runway 18. Tower says, "Cessna 702YS, fly towards the numbers and keep your speed up." What is Tower directing you to do and why?

_____

_____

_____

↓↓ANSWER↓↓

Tower wants you to fly directly towards the threshold of the landing runway while maintaining your cruising airspeed. This maneuver gets you to the runway quickly. It helps increase the spacing between you and the airplane cleared to land after you.

Note: You should not exceed the maximum airspeed for the class of airspace in which you are flying. Begin your speed reduction early enough to permit a stable, on-speed approach and landing.

4. You have just landed and plan to exit the runway. Tower says to you, "Cessna 702YS, I need your best time off the runway." What is Tower directing you to do and why?

_____

_____

↓↓ANSWER↓↓

Tower is telling you to decelerate as quickly as possible to reach a speed at which you can safely exit the runway. By expediting off of the runway, you make the runway available for the airplane on short final approach behind you.

Note: Never compromise safety to expedite off the runway after landing. Decelerate and turn off the runway at a pace that ensures you do not lose control of the aircraft. If Tower has to tell the aircraft landing behind you to go-around because you are still on the runway, the world will not come to an end. If your airplane flips upside down into a ditch next to the runway as you try to exit the runway too quickly, your world might end. Don't do it.

5. You are taxiing on a taxiway parallel to the active runway, heading towards your parking area. Ground says to you, "Cessna 702YS, no delay in your taxi. Traffic is waiting on you." What is Ground directing you to do and why?

_____

_____

↓↓ANSWER↓↓

Ground wants you to speed up your taxi speed so another aircraft does not have to wait longer than necessary to begin its taxi after you pass by.

Note: If you were taxiing slower than normal, speed up, but don't exceed a safe taxi speed.

According to the Pilot/Controller glossary in the AIM, the term "no delay" means you should begin an operation immediately. It does not mean, "go faster" as some pilots _and controllers_ incorrectly believe.

6. You are on a 4-mile straight-in approach to a runway. Tower says to you, "Cessna 702YS, you have 30 knots of overtake on the traffic in front." What is Tower telling you and why?

_____

_____

↓↓ANSWER↓↓

Tower is telling you that you are flying 30 knots faster than the airplane in front of you. He wants you to slow down so you won't get too close to the traffic ahead of you.

7. You are on a 3-mile straight-in approach to a runway. Tower says to you, "Cessna 702YS, plan on the first high-speed turnoff after landing. Traffic is 1-1/2 miles behind you." What is Tower telling you and why?

_____

_____

↓↓ANSWER↓↓

Plan your approach and landing to decelerate in time to make an exit at the first high-speed taxiway turnoff. Failing to do that may require the traffic behind you to go around.

Note: Never adjust your approach, landing, and landing rollout so you feel uncomfortable or compromise safety. Do the best you can, but fly safely. If traffic behind you has to go around, that's just how it has to be.

Think Like an Air Traffic Controller

For all of the following scenarios, you are the local controller ("Tower") at Gainesville Regional Airport, Florida. Your airport has 2 runways. (See the airport diagram below.) The airspace surrounding your airport extends in a 5-mile radius from the center of the airport and runs from the surface up to 2,600 feet MSL. The airport traffic pattern altitude is 1000 feet MSL for single-engine aircraft and 1,500 feet MSL for turbine and heavy aircraft. Runway 11 has an ILS approach system. Airliners must use Runways 11/29, while light aircraft generally use Runways 7/25. (Note: This is an extremely challenging exercise. Do your best but don't worry if you don't get all of answers correct in this section. In many cases, there will be more than one correct answer.)

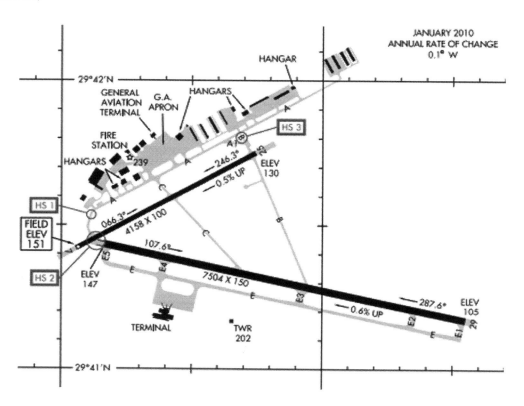

1. You have a Cessna 152 on a midfield left downwind for Runway 7 and a Boeing 737 on a 5-mile final for Runway 11. Left to continue on their own, it is very likely that the Cessna and the 737 will cross paths on final approach with nearly zero separation. You need to delay the Cessna's turn to base leg. Write what you would say to the Cessna 152, call sign Cessna 638EW:

_____

↓↓ANSWER↓↓

"Cessna 638EW, make a right 360. I'll call your base."

Note: You might also tell the Cessna why you are giving him a 360-degree turn: "Traffic is a Boeing 737 on a 5-mile final for Runway 11." A 360 turn is preferable to extending the Cessna's downwind leg. An extended downwind path for Runway 7 intersects the final approach path to Runway 11. You do not want the Cessna and the B-737 to cross paths.

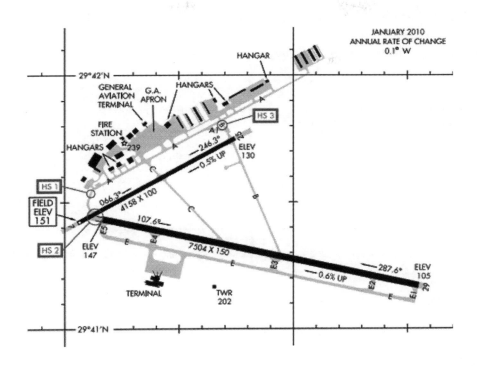

2. The Cessna 638EW (C-152) is still in your pattern, flying touch-and-goes. A Beechcraft 36 Bonanza taxies out on Taxiway A and holds short of Runway 7. The ground controller turns to you and says, "The Bonanza wants to stay in the pattern for touch-and-goes." Just then, the C-152, on takeoff leg from Runway 7, calls, "Cessna 638EW, requests right traffic." The right downwind is clear and there is no one else currently in the traffic pattern. Write your clearance for the C-152:

↓↓ANSWER↓↓

"Cessna 638EW, right traffic approved." Or, "Cessna 638EW, right closed traffic approved."

3. The Bonanza contacts you, "Bonanza 624SL is ready at Runway 7, requesting touch-and-goes." The C-152 is turning from right crosswind to right downwind. If you tell the Bonanza to fly right-hand patterns, it's likely his higher airspeed will cause him to eventually catch up to the C-152. The left downwind is clear and there is no additional aircraft in the airport traffic pattern. Write your clearance to the Bonanza:

"Bonanza 624SL, make left traffic, Runway 7, cleared for takeoff."

4. The Bonanza is now on takeoff leg. The C-152 calls, "Cessna 638EW, right downwind, Runway 7, touch-and-go." Write your clearance for the Cessna:

_____

_____

"Cessna 638EW, Runway 7, cleared touch-and-go."

5. As the Cessna approaches right base leg, the Bonanza calls, "Bonanza 624SL, left downwind, Runway 7, touch-and-go." Spacing between the Bonanza and Cessna looks good enough to allow the Bonanza to follow the Cessna. Write your clearance for the Bonanza:

_____

_____

"Bonanza 624SL, you are number 2 following a Cessna 152 on a right base for Runway 7. Runway 7, cleared touch-and-go."

6. Just as the Cessna touches down on the runway, and the Bonanza is rolling wings level on left base leg for Runway 7, you hear, "Gainesville Tower, Piper 442KN, 10 miles west of the airport, inbound for landing, with information Xray." You would like a position report from the Piper as he enters your class D airspace, which reaches out 5 miles from the center of the airport. Write your reply to the Piper aircraft:

_____

_____

"Piper 442KN, report 5 miles west of the airport."

Note: This is a judgment call. You may also tell the Piper to "Make straight-in for Runway 7" since he is approaching from the west. Almost any answer works here.

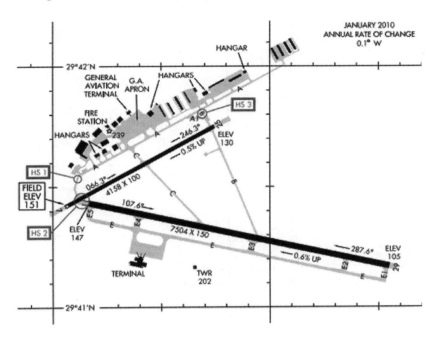

7. The Cessna 152 has completed his touch-and-go and is now on takeoff leg. The Bonanza is just crossing the threshold of Runway 7 for his touch-and-go. The Cessna pilot says, "Cessna 638EW, requests left closed traffic." The left downwind is clear. As the pattern becomes busier, you would like the Cessna pilot to alert you when on a midfield downwind. Write your clearance for the Cessna:

_____

_____

↓↓ANSWER↓↓

"Cessna 638EW, left closed traffic approved. Report a midfield downwind."

8. As the Cessna is about halfway through the left crosswind leg, Bonanza 624SL is on the takeoff leg. If you clear the Bonanza to fly a left-hand pattern, he will surely overtake the Cessna on this circuit. Write your clearance for the Bonanza:

_____

_____

147

"Bonanza 624SL, make right traffic." Or, "Bonanza 624SL, make right closed traffic."

Note: Or, if you wanted to keep the Bonanza in the left-hand pattern for Runway 7, you could say, "Continue on the upwind (takeoff) leg. I'll call your turn to crosswind." This will improve the spacing between the Bonanza and the Cessna.

9. The Cessna 152 reports left downwind for Runway 7. About 10 seconds after that, the Bonanza reports right downwind for Runway 7, full stop. Then you hear, "Piper 442KN is 5 miles west of the airport, full stop." You see the Piper in the distance and can see that he is perfectly lined up for a straight-in approach to Runway 7. Write your clearance for the Piper:

_____

_____

"Piper 442KN, make straight in for Runway 7. Runway 7, cleared to land."

The Piper is now 2 miles out on a straight-in approach to Runway 7. Bonanza 624SL is approaching his turn to right base leg. The Cessna is still on left downwind leg. (See diagram.)

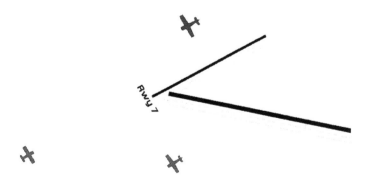

Cessna on left downwind, Bonanza approaching base leg, Piper on 2-mile final.

10. It appears the Bonanza and the Piper may meet on short final approach. You would like to get the Piper on the ground. Write your call to the Bonanza asking him if he sees the Piper Warrior on a 2-mile final:

_____

_____

↓↓**ANSWER** ↓↓

"Bonanza 624SL, you're number 2 behind a Piper Warrior on a 2-mile final. Report that traffic in sight."

11. The pilot of Bonanza says, "Bonanza 624SL, traffic in sight." Write your reply to the Bonanza pilot:

_____

_____

↓↓**ANSWER** ↓↓

"Bonanza 624SL, follow the Piper Warrior, number 2, cleared to land."

12. As the Bonanza turns right base leg, 2 miles from Runway 7, Cessna 638EW approaches his turn to left base leg, 3/4 of a mile from Runway 7. You do not want the Cessna to fly another 2 to 3 miles on an extended downwind to build spacing behind the Bonanza, but you would like to delay his turn to base leg. Write your clearance to the Cessna:

_____

_____

↓↓**ANSWER** ↓↓

"Cessna 628EW, make a right 360 for traffic turning right base."

13. Stepping forward 10 minutes in time, the Bonanza, the Piper and the Cessna have landed and taxied to parking. You now have 5 aircraft waiting to take off on Runway 7. There is a Beechcraft Baron, call sign Baron 8316Y, on a 2-mile final for Runway 7. You ask the first aircraft in line, "Tomahawk 707WQ, can you make an immediate departure?" The pilot answers, "Tomahawk 707WQ, affirmative." Write what you would say to this pilot to clear him to depart immediately:

_____

_____

↓↓ANSWER↓↓

"Tomahawk 707WQ, Runway 7, cleared for an immediate takeoff (or, 'cleared for takeoff, no delay'). Traffic is on a 2-mile final."

14. The Tomahawk begins the takeoff roll. After rolling 100 feet, you notice the Tomahawk stops accelerating. The pilot says, "Tomahawk 707WQ is aborting the takeoff." Baron 8316Y is now only 1/2 mile from landing and the Tomahawk is still several hundred feet from the nearest taxiway turnoff. The Baron will not be able to land on 7 and it's too late to switch his landing runway to Runway 11. Write what you would say to the pilot of the Baron:

_____

_____

↓↓ANSWER↓↓

"Baron 8316Y, go around. Traffic is still on the runway."

Note: From the AIM Pilot/Controller Glossary—"Abort—To terminate a preplanned aircraft maneuver; e.g., an aborted takeoff." The term "rejected" is not in the Pilot/Controller Glossary but is used in the text of the AIM to refer to a discontinued landing. "In the event of a balked (rejected) landing . . ." (AIM 5-4-21 h. Missed Approach.)

When discontinuing a takeoff, the most important step is to stop the aircraft safely on the runway. Transmit your intent to stop to Tower only after the maneuver is well under control. At that point, you can transmit anything that makes it clear to Tower that you are stopping. Expect Tower to ask you if you will be taxiing clear of the runway and whether you require any assistance. Again, do not rush to answer the radio. Concentrate on safe aircraft control. Transmit your intentions after ensuring a safe conclusion to your aborted/discontinued takeoff.

15. The pilot who aborted his takeoff tells you he will taxi clear of the runway and he will not require any assistance. The Baron executes his go-around. He is on takeoff leg. You don't want to delay the Baron any longer, but there are still 4 other aircraft waiting to take off on Runway 7. You decide to have the Baron land on Runway 11 this time. Write your clearance to Baron 8316Y:

_____

_____

↓↓ANSWER↓↓

"Baron 8316Y, make left (or right traffic) for Runway One One."

Flying Into and Out of Class Charlie Airspace

There is an extensive discussion of operations inside Class Charlie airspace in my book, *Radio Mastery for VFR Pilots*. The long and the short of this discussion is you may use what the FAA calls Basic Radar Service for VFR Aircraft when flying in Class C.

1. Are you required to participate in Basic Radar Service for VFR aircraft while operating inside Class C airspace?

Circle the correct answer:

   Yes. No. Maybe.

↓↓ANSWER↓↓

No. (AIM 4-1-18 a. 2. Terminal Radar Service for VFR Aircraft.)

Explanation: Participation in radar service when flying VFR is strictly voluntary.

Before you can make a choice about whether to use radar service, it helps to know what you are getting when you participate:

1. Radar vectoring for sequencing with other participating aircraft.
2. Radar separation from IFR aircraft.
3. Traffic safety advisories and alerts.
4. Terrain and obstruction alerts, if you ask for that part of the service.

2. Even if you choose not to participate in Basic Radar Service within Class C airspace, you must still have what equipment on your aircraft in order to enter Class C?

_____

_____

↓↓ANSWER↓↓

A working transponder and a working radio. (AIM 3-2-4 c. 2. Class C Airspace.)

Note: You may enter Class C without a working transponder if you receive a one-time waiver from the FAA.

Let's hit the highlights of Class C radio work by covering a few questions.

3. When you choose to participate in radar service in Class C, will ATC give you headings to fly to put you in the sequence for the landing runway?

Circle the correct answer:

Yes. No. Maybe.

↓↓ANSWER↓↓

Yes. (AIM 4-1-18 a. 1. d. Terminal Radar Service for VFR Aircraft.)

4. When departing an airport within Class C, will ATC assign headings to your aircraft to maintain separation from other participating aircraft as you proceed outbound?

Circle the correct answer:

Yes. No. Maybe.

↓↓ANSWER↓↓

No. (AIM 4-1-18 a. 5. Terminal Radar Service for VFR Aircraft.)

Explanation: ATC is not required to maintain specific standards of separation for VFR aircraft within Class C airspace. ATC will provide IFR aircraft with standard separation from all other aircraft. However, ATC will give you traffic advisories and *suggested* headings to avoid other aircraft.

5. Will ATC assign specific airspeeds to participating VFR aircraft?

Circle the correct answer:

Yes. No. Maybe.

↓↓**ANSWER** ↓↓

No. (AIM 4-1-18 Terminal Radar Service for VFR Aircraft.)

6. Will ATC assign specific altitudes to VFR aircraft?

Circle the correct answer:

Yes. No. Maybe.

↓↓**ANSWER** ↓↓

Maybe.

Explanation: ATC may say, "Maintain at or above" a specific altitude to ensure safety or for convenience in sequencing traffic. ATC will not assign specific altitudes to VFR aircraft in order to maintain vertical separation from other aircraft. In most cases, altitude control is left to the discretion of the pilot flying VFR.

Essentially, when operating in VFR in Class C under radar direction, you are still responsible for management of you airplane's airspeed and altitude. ATC will use only headings to place you in sequence.

If you choose not to participate in Basic Radar Service, after establishing contact with the Class C's radar controller, you will be told to switch to the appropriate airport tower frequency, if inbound for landing. If you choose not to participate and you are departing from an airport in Class C, the radar controller will provide flight following service only until you exit his airspace.

7. Fill in the blank. The edge of Class C usually begins _____ nautical miles from the center of the primary airport served by Class C.

↓↓**ANSWER** ↓↓

10. (AIM 3-2-4 Class C Airspace.)

Note: The exact dimensions of the airspace may vary widely by airport. Refer to your sectional chart or terminal area chart for individual coverage of each Class C airspace.

8. Regardless of the shape and size of a Class C airspace, all Class C operations have something called an Outer Area. What is the Outer Area?

_____

_____

↓↓**ANSWER** ↓↓

The Outer Area is the limit of a radar approach control's airspace. It extends in a 20-mile radius from the center of the Class C's primary airport. (AIM Pilot/Controller Glossary.)

Let's practice. Your call sign is Lancair 736HX. You are inbound to the Akron-Canton Airport, Ohio (KCAK). (See the airport diagram.)

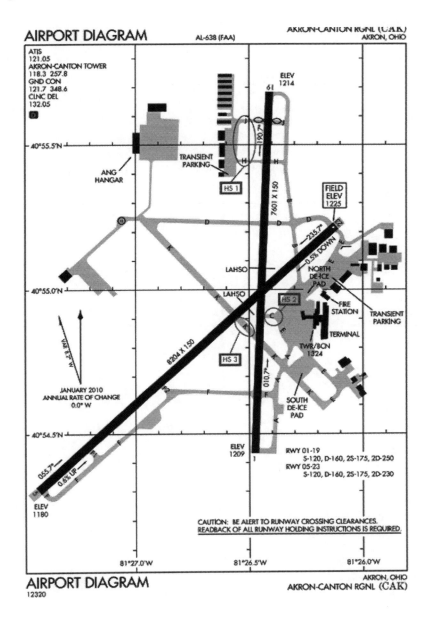

Twenty-five miles southwest of the airport, you terminate VFR flight following with Cleveland Center and switch to Akron-Canton Approach's frequency. You are now 22 miles southwest of the airport at 3,500 feet MSL.

9. You previously listened to the airport's ATIS and wrote the information identifier down as "C." The sky condition at the airport is clear and 10 miles visibility. The wind is 360 at 10. The airport is using Runway 1 for landings and departures. Write what you would say to establish contact with Akron-Canton Approach:

_____

_____

↓↓**ANSWER**↓↓

"Akron-Canton Approach, Lancair 736HX, 22 miles southwest of the airport, inbound for landing Akron-Canton with (information) Charlie."

(headset icon) Now, say it out loud:

Note: It's important to say the name of the airport where you intend to land. Some approach control facilities handle traffic for multiple airports.

10. The Approach controller says, "Lancair 736HX, Akron-Canton Approach, squawk 0571." Write what you would say in reply:

_____

_____

↓↓ANSWER↓↓

"Lancair 736HX. 0571."

(headset icon) Now, say it out loud:

Trivia: Approach control will always assign a transponder code that begins with a zero to VFR aircraft.

11. Approach says, "Lancair 6HX, radar contact 20 miles southwest of Akron-Canton. Expect Runway 1. Maintain VFR." Write your readback:

_____

_____

↓↓ANSWER↓↓

"Lancair 6HX."

(headset icon) Now, say it out loud:

Explanation: The controller switched to an abbreviated call sign, so you may also. There are no clearances in Approach's radio call to you. The entire transmission is advisory information, so there is no need to repeat any of it.

12. Approach says, "Lancair 6HX, turn left, heading zero four zero." Write your readback:

_____

_____

↓↓**ANSWER**↓↓

"Lancair 6HX, left heading zero four zero."

Now, say it out loud:

Explanation: Be sure to include the turn direction, the word "heading" and the numbers.

13. Approach says, "Lancair 6HX, traffic is a Citation, 1 to 2 o'clock and 5 miles northbound at 7,000, descending." You do not see the Citation. Write your reply to Approach:

_____

_____

↓↓**ANSWER**↓↓

"Lancair 6HX, negative contact."

Now, say it out loud:

14. Now 10 miles from the airport, Approach says, "Lancair 6HX, turn right heading zero seven zero, vectors for sequencing behind a King Air, your 10 o'clock and 4 miles, 4,000." As you enter the turn and begin descending, you do not see the King Air. Write your readback to Approach:

_____

_____

↓↓**ANSWER**↓↓

"Lancair 6HX, right heading zero seven zero. Negative contact."

Now, say it out loud:

Explanation: This is a short and simple reply to a long, complicated transmission from ATC. All you need to do is readback the clearance, and tell the controller you are looking for the traffic.

15. You begin a descent to traffic pattern altitude (2,200 MSL). Write the radio call you would make:

_____

↓↓**ANSWER** ↓↓

"Lancair 6HX is descending to traffic pattern altitude (or, 'descending to 2,200')."

16. Now you see the King Air at your 9 o'clock position, slightly high. Write your radio call to Approach:

"Lancair 6HX, traffic in sight."

🎧 Now, say it out loud:

Explanation: It's important to let ATC know when you see this traffic because it is the traffic you will be following to the airport.

17. Approach says, "Lancair 6HX, roger, turn left heading zero tree zero. The airport is at your 10 to 11 o'clock and eight miles. Report the airport in sight." You see the airport. Write your readback to Approach:

_____

↓↓**ANSWER** ↓↓

"Lancair 6HX, left heading zero tree zero. Airport in sight."

🎧 Now, say it out loud:

18. Approach says, "Lancair 6HX, contact Akron-Canton Tower on 118.3."

Write your reply to Approach:

_____

↓↓**ANSWER** ↓↓

"Lancair 6HX, 118.3."

Now, say it out loud:

19. You have switched frequencies to Tower. Runway 1 is now 11 o'clock and 6 miles to your north. Write your radio call to the tower controller:

_____

_____

"Akron-Canton Tower, Lancair 736HX, 6 miles south of the airport."

Now, say it out loud:

20. The tower controller says, "Lancair 736HX, Akron-Canton Tower, make a straight-in for Runway 1 and report 3 miles. You are number 3." Write your readback to Tower:

_____

_____

"Lancair 736HX, we'll report a 3-mile straight-in for Runway 1."

Now, say it out loud:

21. You are now on a 3-mile straight-in approach to Runway 1. The King Air in front of you has landed and is turning off the runway. You see a high-wing airplane turning onto final approach, about 1 mile from the runway. Write your radio call to Tower:

_____

_____

"Lancair 736HX, 3 miles straight-in, Runway 1."

Now, say it out loud:

22. Tower says, "Lancair 736HX, Runway 1, cleared to land. Traffic is a Cessna 172 rolling out on final." Write your readback to Tower:

_____

_____

↓↓**ANSWER**↓↓

"Lancair 736HX, Runway 1, cleared to land. Traffic in sight."

Now, say it out loud:

23. You have landed and Tower says, "Lancair 6HX, any right turn off the runway. Contact Ground, .7 when clear." Write your reply to Tower:

_____

_____

↓↓**ANSWER**↓↓

"Lancair 6HX, any right turn. Ground .7 when clear."

Now, say it out loud:

Departing from an airport in Class C

When departing from an airport in Class C airspace, you will need a transponder code and a frequency assigned for the departure controller. At airports inside Class C, you can pick up your transponder code and departure frequency from a person in the control tower manning a position called Clearance Delivery.

If the airport is busy enough, and the airport has the budget to have a third person in the control tower, the Clearance Delivery position may be manned by a third controller. Otherwise, Clearance Delivery is usually handled by the ground controller. Depending on the budget, the time of day, and the amount of traffic at the airport, the tower may be manned by only one person. That person will manage all three positions: Ground,

Tower, and Clearance Delivery.

To get a pre-departure clearance, simply dial in the Clearance Delivery frequency and tell the controller what you plan to do. Be sure to include the current ATIS identifier when making initial contact with Clearance Delivery. If there is no separate frequency for Clearance Delivery, dial in the frequency stated in the airport NOTAMs or as indicated in the ATIS broadcast. For example, "All aircraft contact Ground on 121.9 for Clearance Delivery."

Today, your call sign is Mooney 211VR. You are flying a Mooney Mk20 from Akron-Canton Airport (KCAK), Ohio on a VFR flight to the Genesee County Airport (KGCQ) in Batavia, New York. Your planned cruising altitude will be 7,500 as you travel northeast near the southern shore of Lake Erie.

The current Akron-Canton ATIS code is "H." The airport is using Runway 1 for departures. You are parked on the Transient Ramp at the north end of the airport. (See the airport diagram below.)

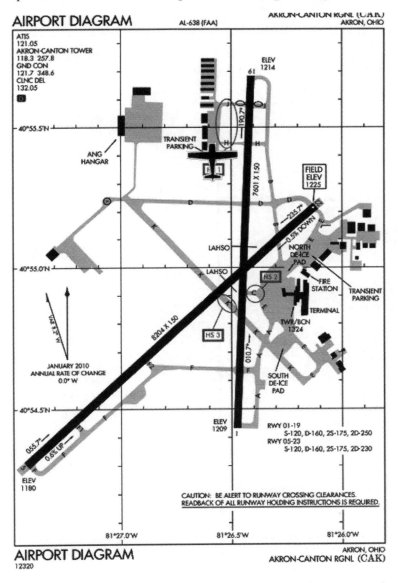

1. Write your radio call for making initial contact with Akron-Canton Clearance Delivery:

_____

"Akron-Canton Clearance, Mooney 211VR, with information Hotel, VFR to the northeast."

🎧 Now, say it out loud:

Explanation: Once you leave the Class C airspace under VFR, ATC does not care about your flight plan or destination. All the controller wants to know is what general direction you'll be heading as you fly through his airspace.

2. Clearance Delivery says, "Mooney 211VR, Akron-Canton Clearance, departure frequency will be 125.5, squawk 0250, and say your position on the airport." Write your readback to Clearance Delivery:

_____

_____

"Mooney 211VR, 125.5, 0250, and we are parked on the Transient Ramp."

🎧 Now, say it out loud:

Explanation: When reading back your clearance from Clearance Delivery, you only need to repeat the numbers.

3. Clearance Delivery says, "Mooney 211VR, contact Ground on .7 when ready to taxi." You have started your engine and you are now ready to taxi. With Ground Control tuned on your radio, write your initial radio call to the ground controller:

_____

_____

"Mooney 211VR is ready to taxi."

🎧 Now, say it out loud:

Explanation: No need to repeat the ATIS code unless it has changed. If Clearance Delivery asked for your parking position, that controller will pass the information to the ground controller, so no need to repeat that either.

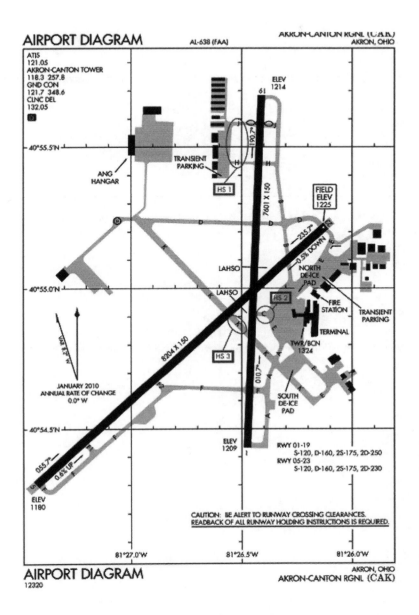

4. The ground controller says, "Mooney 211VR, Akron-Canton Ground, Runway 1, taxi via Hotel and hold short of Runway 1." First, write your taxi clearance in note form:

_____

↓↓**ANSWER**↓↓

1 H/1

5. Next, write your readback to Ground:

_____

"Mooney 1VR, Runway 1, taxi via Hotel and hold short of Runway 1."

🎧 Now, say it out loud:

6. Ground says, "Mooney 211VR, monitor Tower on 118.3." Write your reply to Ground:

_____

_____

"Mooney 211VR, 118.3."

🎧 Now, say it out loud:

7. After switching to Tower's frequency, should you make a radio call to Tower?

Circle the correct answer:

Yes. No. Maybe.

No.

Explanation: The ground controller told you to monitor Tower's frequency.

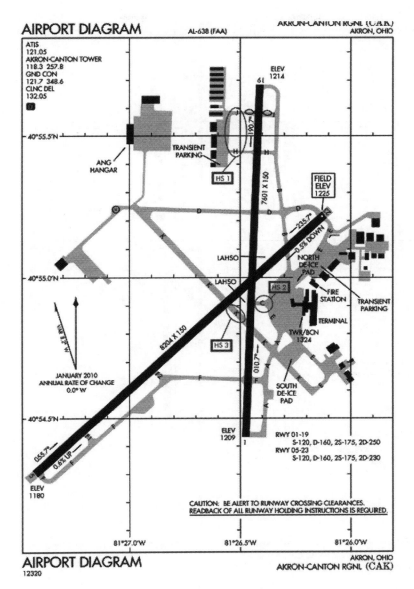

AIRPORT DIAGRAM   AL-638 (FAA)   AKRON-CANTON RGNL (CAK)
AKRON, OHIO

AIRPORT DIAGRAM
12320

AKRON, OHIO
AKRON-CANTON RGNL (CAK)

8. Tower says, "Mooney 211VR, Akron-Canton Tower, at Hotel, cross Runway 1 and make the right turn onto Bravo. Contact Ground .7 after you cross." Write your taxi clearance in note form:

↓↓ANSWER↓↓

x1 RB .7

Note: If Tower says, "Without delay, cross Runway 1 . . ." don't waste time writing notes. Make the crossing and try to commit the rest to memory. If you forget what to do after crossing, *clear the runway*, then ask Ground what to do next after switching frequencies.

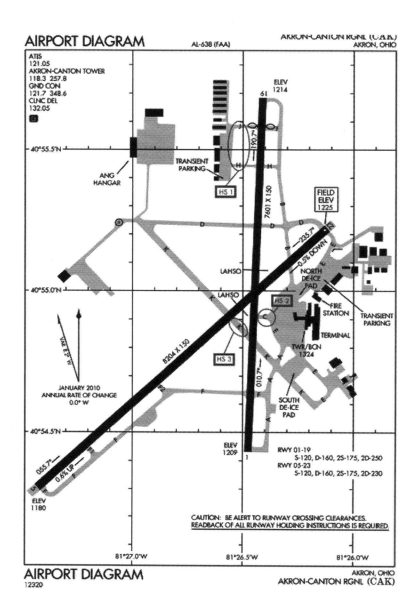

9. Write your readback to Tower:

_____

_____

↓↓ANSWER↓↓

"Mooney 211VR, at Hotel, cross Runway 1. Right on Bravo. Point 7 after crossing."

🎧 Now, say it out loud:

10. You have crossed Runway 1 and you are now turning onto Taxiway Bravo. Should you make a radio call to Ground, or monitor his frequency?

Circle the correct answer:

Make the call.   Monitor.

↓↓ANSWER↓↓

Make the call.

11. What is your call to Ground as you turn onto Taxiway Bravo?

_____

↓↓ANSWER↓↓

"Akron-Canton Ground, Mooney 211VR, on Bravo."

12. Ground says, "Mooney 1VR, continue via Bravo. Cross Runway 5 and right on Echo. Hold short of Taxiway Alpha."

Write your taxi clearance in note form:

↓↓ANSWER↓↓

B x 5 RE/A

13. Write your reply to Ground:

_____

↓↓ANSWER↓↓

"Mooney 1VR, continue Bravo. Cross Runway 5 Right Echo. Hold short of Alpha."

Now, say it out loud:

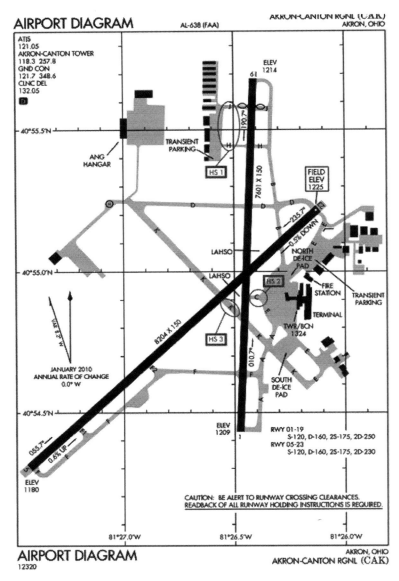

AIRPORT DIAGRAM

AL-638 (FAA)

AKRON-CANTON RGNL (CAK)
AKRON, OHIO

ATIS
121.05
AKRON-CANTON TOWER
118.3 257.8
GND CON
121.7 348.6
CLNC DEL
132.05

CAUTION: BE ALERT TO RUNWAY CROSSING CLEARANCES.
READBACK OF ALL RUNWAY HOLDING INSTRUCTIONS IS REQUIRED.

AIRPORT DIAGRAM
12320

AKRON, OHIO
AKRON-CANTON RGNL (CAK)

14. You taxi south on Bravo and make the right turn onto Taxiway Echo. Approaching the intersection of Taxiways Echo and Alpha, you come to a stop. As you wait on Taxiway Echo, you see a Beech 1900 turboprop turn from Taxiway Kilo onto Taxiway Alpha. The turboprop crosses in front of you as it continues toward the airport's passenger terminal. Then Ground says to you, "Mooney 1VR, continue right on Alpha. Contact Tower on 118.3 when ready." Write your readback to Ground. (No need for notes this time. The clearance is simple.)

_____

_____

↓↓**ANSWER**↓↓

"Mooney 1VR, right Alpha. Tower when ready."

🎧 Now, say it out loud:

Explanation: This is the fourth time you have heard Tower's frequency. There is no need to read back frequencies that you know well.

Tower did not tell you to hold short of Runway 1 because a clearance to an assigned runway is not a clearance to enter the runway. You may not enter any runway, active or closed, without a specific clearance from ATC to enter that runway. (AIM 4-3-18 a. 6. Taxiing.)

15. On Taxiway Alpha, holding short of Runway 1, you complete your pre-departure checks. Then you switch to Tower's frequency. Write your radio call to Tower:

_____

_____

↓↓ANSWER↓↓

"Akron-Canton Tower, Mooney 211VR, ready at Runway 1."

🎧 Now, say it out loud:

Explanation: Although you have talked to Tower before, this is a new contact. Go back to your full call sign. Be sure to state the Tower's name as well to make sure you are talking to the correct person.

16. Tower says, "Mooney 211VR, hold short of Runway 1." Write your readback to Tower:

_____

_____

↓↓ANSWER↓↓

"Mooney 211VR, hold short of Runway 1."

🎧 Now, say it out loud:

17. As you hold short, you see a Westwind business jet land on Runway 1. As the Westwind touches down on the runway, Tower says to you, "Mooney 211VR, Runway 1, line up and wait. Be ready to go. Traffic is a Learjet, 4 miles out." First, in your own words, what is Tower telling you to do?

_____

_____

↓↓ANSWER↓↓

Enter the runway and stop. Be prepared to begin a takeoff roll as soon as Tower clears you for takeoff.

18. Write your readback to Tower:

_____

_____

↓↓ANSWER↓↓

"Mooney 211VR, Runway 1, line up and wait."

🎧 Now, say it out loud:

19. You turn onto the runway and stop just as the Westwind is turning off the runway. Tower says, "Mooney 211VR, I'll have a turn for you in the air. Runway 1, cleared for takeoff." Write your readback to Tower:

_____

_____

↓↓ANSWER↓↓

"Mooney 211VR, Runway 1, cleared for takeoff."

🎧 Now, say it out loud:

20. Without directions for what to do immediately after takeoff, what heading should you fly after liftoff from the runway?

_____

↓↓**ANSWER**↓↓

Runway heading, or the published standard heading for the runway in use.

Explanation: Published headings can be found either in the airport's NOTAMs or in the ATIS.

21. You are now airborne and climbing through 500 feet above the airport elevation. Tower says, "Mooney 211VR, turn right, heading zero eight zero." Write your reply to Tower:

_____

_____

↓↓**ANSWER**↓↓

"Mooney 211VR, right heading zero eight zero."

🎧 Now, say it out loud:

22. As you roll out on your 080-degree heading, Tower says, "Mooney 211VR, contact Departure." Why didn't Tower give you Departure Control's frequency?

_____

_____

↓↓**ANSWER**↓↓

You already have the correct departure frequency to use because Clearance Delivery gave it to you earlier.

23. You switch to Departure Control's frequency. You are now passing 2,400 feet MSL, enroute to a cruising altitude of 7,500 feet MSL. Write your radio call to Departure:

↓↓ANSWER↓↓

"Akron-Canton Departure, Mooney 211VR, leaving 2,400. Climbing to 7,500."

🎧 Now, say it out loud:

Explanation: No need to advise the departure controller that you are flying VFR. That information was entered into the ATC system when you called Clearance Delivery.

So there is absolutely no doubt about how to state your current and intended altitude when checking in with ATC, here is the direct quote from the AIM on the subject:

"**(a)** When operating in a radar environment: On initial contact, the pilot should inform the controller of the aircraft's assigned altitude preceded by the words "level," or "climbing to," or "descending to," as appropriate; and the aircraft's present vacating altitude, if applicable." (AIM 5-3-1.)

An early edition of *Radio Mastery for VFR Pilots* had a different method for stating altitudes upon initial contact with ATC. Later editions of the book were adjusted to coincide with the guidance in the AIM.

24. Departure says, "Mooney 211VR, Akron-Canton Departure, radar contact. Climbing to 7,500. Maintain VFR and advise me before you change your cruising altitude." Write your reply to Departure:

↓↓ANSWER↓↓

"Mooney 211VR."

🎧 Now, say it out loud:

Note: You could add, "We'll advise before we change cruising altitude," but simply saying your call sign acknowledges everything.

25. Departure says, "Attention all aircraft. The new Akron-Canton ATIS is India. Altimeter two niner, niner fife." Do you need to reply to this transmission?

Yes. No. Maybe.

↓↓ANSWER↓↓

No.

Explanation: You should not reply to general broadcasts. Only reply to information directed to your call sign. There are specific instances when the change in ATIS information is extremely important. In that case, ATC will direct each aircraft on the frequency to acknowledge the change. ATC may do this with a roll call using each aircraft's call sign, or ATC may tell all aircraft on the frequency to acknowledge simultaneously with a transponder ident.

26. Departure says to you, "Mooney 1VR, traffic 1 o'clock and 10 miles, southwest bound, type and altitude unknown." You do not see the traffic. Write your reply to Departure:

_____

_____

↓↓ANSWER↓↓

"Mooney 1VR, negative contact."

Now, say it out loud:

27. Departure says, "Mooney 1VR, previously reported traffic now 12 o'clock and 5 miles, opposite direction, altitude unknown. It appears to be slow moving. Would you like a vector around that traffic?" You do not see the traffic and would like an avoidance vector. Write your reply to Departure:

_____

_____

↓↓ANSWER↓↓

"Mooney 1VR, will take the vector." Or, "Mooney 1VR, affirmative."

Now, say it out loud:

28. Departure says, "Mooney 1VR, turn right heading zero niner zero and let me know if you spot the traffic." Write your reply to Departure:

_____

_____

↓↓ANSWER↓↓

"Mooney 1VR, right heading zero niner zero. We'll report the traffic in sight."

Now, say it out loud:

29. Departure says, "Mooney 1VR, previously reported traffic should now be off your left side, and 2 miles, altitude unknown." You search your 9 o'clock and spot a helicopter at what you estimate to be less than 1,000 above the ground. Write your radio call to Departure:

_____

_____

↓↓ANSWER↓↓

"Mooney 1VR has the traffic in sight. It appears to be a helicopter at about 1,000 feet."

Now, say it out loud:

30. Departure says, "Mooney 1VR, thanks for that report. Traffic is no factor. Resume own navigation on course." Write your reply to Departure:

_____

_____

↓↓ANSWER↓↓

"Mooney 1VR, resuming own nav on course."

Now, say it out loud:

31. About 20 miles from the airport, Departure says, "Mooney 1VR, no observed traffic in your vicinity. Radar service terminated. Squawk 1200. For further flight following, suggest Cleveland Center on 120.77." Write your reply to Departure:

_____

_____

↓↓ANSWER↓↓

"Mooney 1VR, squawking 1200 and switching, 120.77."

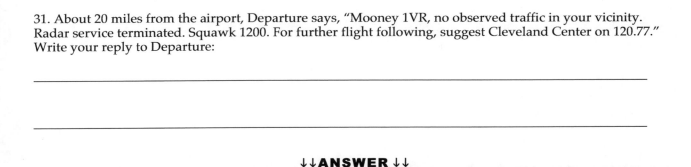 Now, say it out loud:

Note: Saying you will squawk 1200 is technique only. ATC will be able to see your radar datablock switch to 1200 when you make the change in your transponder.

Think Like an Air Traffic Controller

Class C airspace is controlled by people in a Terminal Radar Approach Control Facility (TRACON). Within the facility there are usually 2 or more radar control positions that control segments of the airspace around the airport at the center of Class C. At many airports the airspace is divided into hemispheres. Who you talk to at the TRACON depends on which hemisphere your flight path passes through.

Sometimes, each sector of a TRACON will be further divided into separate departure and arrival control positions. More often, a single controller will handle both departures and arrivals in his sector. It is not unusual for the person you refer to on the radio as Approach to also be called Departure by other aircraft. The difference in labels helps the controller keep the airplanes on his screen mentally sorted into arrivals and departures. Additionally, specialized symbols on the controller's radar display also help him sort arrivals and departures.

For the following scenarios, you will be playing the role of Approach and Departure Control in the western hemisphere of Class C airspace surrounding Baton Rouge Metropolitan/Ryan Field Airport, Louisiana (KBTR). It's a VFR day at the airport with clear skies and unlimited visibility. Ryan Tower is using Runway 4L for turbojet and large turboprop arrivals and departures and Runway 4R for light aircraft. The current ATIS code is "W." The surface wind is 020 at 15. The current altimeter is 30.04.

You have just cleared an MD-90, inbound to the airport, to descend and maintain 5,000. Before the pilot of the MD-90 can reply, you hear the following on your frequency: "Baton Rouge Approach, Piper 569GL, one fife miles west, inbound for landing." You say, "Piper 569GL, standby," and then the MD-90 reads back his clearance to descend. (See illustration.)

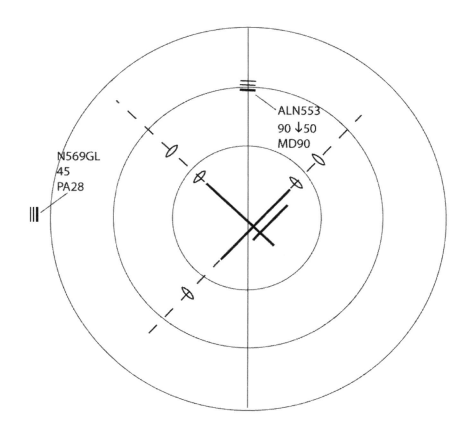

1. Given the circumstances, would you expect Piper 569GL to remain outside of your Class C airspace or will he continue to enter the Class C?

Circle the correct answer:

He will remain outside. He will enter.

↓↓**ANSWER** ↓↓

He will enter.

2. You call the pilot of Piper 569GL again and assign a squawk code to his transponder. There are quite a few other radar targets 15 miles west of the airport. What could you say to the Piper pilot to get him to highlight his aircraft on your radar display?

↓↓**ANSWER** ↓↓

"Piper 569GL, ident."

3. With regard to cloud clearances and inflight visibility, what are you required to say to Piper 569GL as an advisory?

_____

↓↓**ANSWER**↓↓

"Piper 569GL, maintain VFR."

4. As a controller of Class C airspace, are you allowed to give a clearance that requires a VFR aircraft to descend or climb to a specific altitude?

Circle the correct answer:

Yes. No. Maybe.

↓↓**ANSWER**↓↓

No.

Explanation: You may assign altitudes to keep VFR aircraft clear of obstacles, traffic patterns, or restricted/prohibited airspace. Separating aircraft by altitude does not apply to VFR aircraft.

5. As a controller of Class C airspace, are you allowed to give a clearance that requires a VFR aircraft to maintain a specific airspeed?

Circle the correct answer:

Yes. No. Maybe.

↓↓**ANSWER**↓↓

No.

6. What should you say to a pilot of a VFR aircraft that will alert you when the pilot decides to climb or descend?

_____

_____

↓↓**ANSWER**↓↓

"Advise me of any altitude changes." Or, "Advise me before changing altitudes."

You now have Piper 569GL in radar contact at 4,500 feet MSL, 12 miles due west of the airport, heading 090 degrees. Your plan is to set the airplane up for an entry to a right (east) downwind leg to Runway 4R where light aircraft are handled. The best way to do this is to direct the airplane to cross over the center of the airport above the flow of traffic in the airport pattern. This will keep him out of the way of aircraft landing or departing on 4L and 4R as he moves into the east side. (See illustration.)

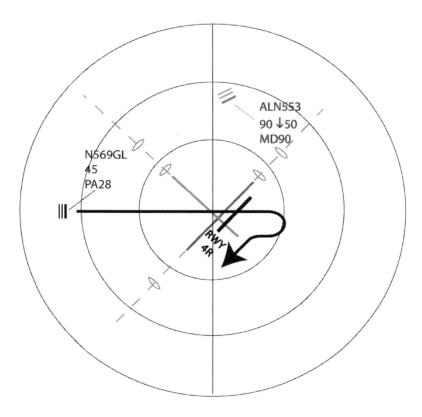

7. If Piper 569GL is currently bearing 270 degrees from the center of the airport and you want him to fly directly over the center of the airport, write the clearance you would give the pilot. He is currently heading 070 degrees. (You may use his abbreviated call sign.)

_____

_____

↓↓**ANSWER** ↓↓

"Piper 9GL, turn right, heading zero niner zero."

Explanation: An airplane bearing 270 degrees is due west of the airport's center. To get an airplane to fly directly towards the airport's center you assign a heading that is the reciprocal of 270 degrees. The reciprocal heading is 090 degrees. (This assumes you do not have to adjust the airplane's heading to compensate for drift caused by winds aloft.)

8. Write the clearance you would give Piper 9GL to keep him at least 500 feet above the airport traffic pattern at as he crosses over Ryan Field. The airport traffic pattern altitude is 1,000 MSL.

_____

_____

↓↓ANSWER↓↓

"Piper 9GL, maintain VFR at or above 1,500."

Note: All ATC assigned altitudes are expressed in feet above MSL. ATC never says "feet" or "MSL" in an altitude clearance because those elements are implied in the clearance.

Exercise continues, next page.

A Boeing 737 has just checked in with you on the descent from the north. You will be directing the 737 toward the south end of your airspace to set him up for a straight-in approach to Runway 4L. You have cleared the 737 to descend and maintain 4,000. The Piper is currently 7 miles west of the airport, maintaining 3,500. The 737 is at the Piper's 10 o'clock position, currently 10 miles distant, heading southbound, descending through 6,000. (See illustration.)

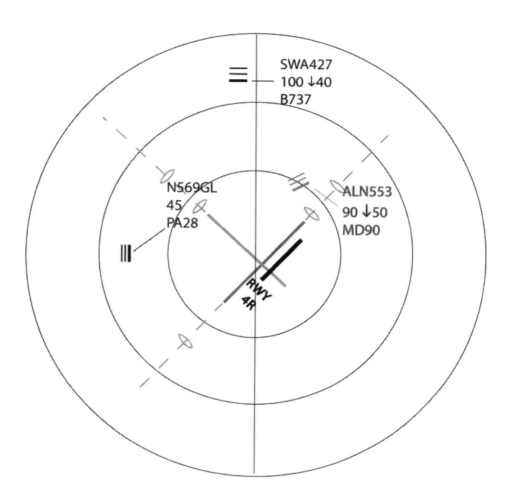

9. Write the radio call you would make to Piper 569GL, advising him of the 737 traffic:

_____

_____

↓↓**ANSWER**↓↓

"Piper 9GL, traffic is a Boeing 737, 10 o'clock and one zero miles, descending through 6,000 for 4,000."

10. The Piper is now 3 miles west of the airport, about to cross into the eastern hemisphere of the Class C airspace. Local procedure says you should switch the airplane over to the approach controller working the east side of the Class C. That controller's frequency is 126.5. Write the radio call you would make to Piper 9GL to push him to the other Baton Rouge approach controller's frequency:

_____

_____

↓↓**ANSWER**↓↓

"Piper 9GL, contact Baton Rouge Approach on 126.5."

Just after the Piper leaves your frequency, a radar target appears on your radar display showing "N7936Z" directly off the departure end of Runway 31. The display also shows the target at 500 feet, climbing. You check your aircraft fight plan strips and see this airplane is a Grumman AA5A (Cheetah), VFR, departing to the northwest. (See illustration.)

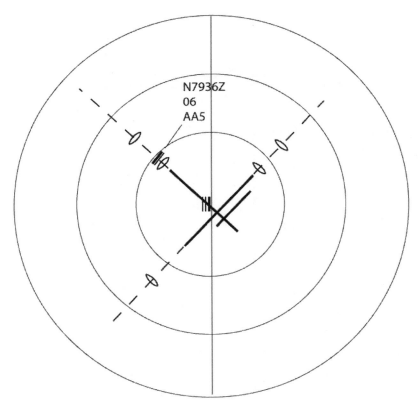

11. The pilot checks in: "Baton Rouge Departure, Grumman 7936Z, leaving 600, climbing to 8,500." You check your radar display at the moment the pilot says his altitude. Your altitude readout at that moment was 600 feet. The airspace to the northwest presently has only one aircraft in it, 18 miles from the airport, heading outbound. There is no reason to assign a specific heading to this aircraft. It would be best to let the pilot

181

proceed on his own navigation as he departs the area. Write your radio call to this pilot:

_____

_____

↓↓**ANSWER**↓↓

"Grumman 7936Z, radar contact. Maintain VFR and advise me if you change your cruising altitude."

12. As Grumman 7936Z approaches the 20-mile limit of the Outer Area around your airspace, you have time to coordinate a handoff to Houston Center. You contact Houston Center's Lafayette sector on your landline and advise him of the VFR aircraft headed his way. The Center controller tells you he's ready for the aircraft. The frequency for Houston Center in that sector is 126.35. Write the radio call you would make to the pilot to push him to Houston Center:

_____

_____

↓↓**ANSWER**↓↓

"Grumman 7936Z, contact Houston Center on 126.35."

Emergencies

There is an old bit of wisdom in the airline industry that says a pilot should never make an announcement using certain words that begin with an "F". These verbal no-no's are: fuel, fire, fog, or the harsh word that some people use to describe sexual congress. Additionally, one old captain jokingly suggested you should never use the word "final" when speaking to passengers because that word is associated with death.

In this section, we are going to cover 4 of the 5 no-nos. We will also cover one emergency that does not begin with an F--a medical emergency--and the semi-emergency of getting lost.

Fuel

1. You are inbound for landing at the Central Wisconsin Airport in a Diamond DA-20. Your call sign is Diamond 703DN. You have determined that you have just enough fuel remaining to arrive at the airport traffic pattern and fit into the normal flow of traffic for a full stop landing. However, if Tower creates any type of delay for you, such as asking you to circle outside of the Class D airspace, you might run out of fuel. Write the radio call you should make to CWA Tower upon initial contact, which alerts the controller you cannot accept any delay in your approach and landing. (You are currently 10 miles north of the airfield.)

_____

_____

↓↓ANSWER↓↓

"CWA Tower, Diamond 703DN, 10 miles north for landing. Minimum fuel." (AIM 5-5-15 Minimum Fuel Advisory.)

🎧 Now, say it out loud:

2. New day, same airport, same airplane, same position. This time, as you fly toward the airport, you realize you are almost out of fuel. To avoid running out of fuel before landing, you will need to cut in front of any other aircraft in the airport's traffic pattern and fly directly to a short final approach. Write the radio call you should make to Tower to give your aircraft priority for landing, given your current fuel state:

_____

_____

↓↓ANSWER↓↓

"CWA Tower, Diamond 703DN, 10 miles north for landing. Emergency fuel."

🎧 Now, say it out loud:

3. When you declare an emergency for any reason, ATC will need to know how much fuel is remaining in your tanks. Why does ATC need this information?

↓↓ANSWER↓↓

Primarily to know how much time you have remaining to work on your emergency before you must land. Secondarily, the airport's fire chief needs to know how much of a fuel load he will be dealing with in the event of a crash. (AIM 6-3-2 Obtaining Emergency Assistance.)

While you may measure your airplane's fuel capacity in gallons or liters, ATC needs to know how much fuel you have remaining measured in hours and minutes. With that in mind, let's run through some examples for practice.

4. You are flying Piper 5336H, burning fuel at a rate of 12 gallons per hour during cruise flight. Your left wing tank has 7 usable gallons remaining and your right wing tank has 9 usable gallons remaining. When ATC asks you how much fuel you have remaining, what would you tell the controller?

↓↓ANSWER↓↓

"Piper 5336H has 1 hour plus two zero remaining."

Explanation: 16 gallons remaining / 12 gallons per hour = 1.33 hours or 1 hour plus 20 minutes.

5. You are flying a twin-engine aircraft. Each engine burns fuel during cruise at a rate of 15 gallons per hour. Your left wing tank has 22 usable gallons remaining. Your right wing tank has 18 usable gallons remaining. Your center tank has 4 usable gallons remaining. When ATC asks you how much fuel you have remaining, what would you tell the controller? Your call sign is Twin Cessna 421LJ.

↓↓ANSWER↓↓

"Twin Cessna 421LJ has 1 hour plus 28 minutes remaining."

Explanation: 44 gallons remaining / 30 gallons per hour = 1.47 hours or 1 hour plus 28 minutes remaining. Note: 1 + 30 would be close enough for an estimate.

Fire

Of all of the types of emergencies you may encounter in your airplane, arguably none is more urgent than an uncontrollable onboard fire. When fire breaks out and you cannot extinguish it, you need to get on the ground as soon as possible.

1. Today you are flying solo in a Bellanca Citabria over southwestern Indiana, near Evansville. You are practicing stalls when all of a sudden you smell smoke in the cockpit. About 10 seconds later, you see black smoke in the cockpit and your aircraft's engine starts running rough. You troubleshoot the problem for a minute but instead of getting better, the smoke intensity is increasing. You check your distance to the nearest airport and see that you are only 15 miles south of the Evansville Regional Airport. You set your transponder code to 7700. Next, you dial in the frequency for Evansville Approach Control and make a radio call. Write the radio call you would make to ATC, using your call sign N486UA:

_____

_____

↓↓ANSWER↓↓

"Evansville Approach, N486UA, one fife miles south of Evansville, declaring an emergency." Or, "Mayday, mayday, mayday, N486UA, one fife miles south of Evansville."

🎧 Now, say it out loud:

2. The Evansville Approach controller says, "N486UA, Evansville Approach, squawk 0673 and state your aircraft type and the nature of your emergency." Write your reply to ATC:

↓↓ANSWER↓↓

"N486UA is a Bellanca Citabria with smoke in the cockpit and a rough-running engine."

🎧 Now, say it out loud:

3. Evansville Approach says, "N6UA, I copy your emergency. Evansville Regional is one o'clock and one two miles. Say your intentions." Write your reply to ATC:

_____

_____

↓↓ANSWER↓↓

"N6UA would like to land immediately at Evansville."

🎧 Now, say it out loud:

4. The controller replies, "N6UA, turn right heading tree six zero, vectors to the airport. As able, I'll need your fuel remaining and number of people onboard." You have 38 usable liters of fuel remaining with a fuel burn rate of 30.3 liters per hour. Write your reply to ATC:

_____

_____

↓↓ANSWER↓↓

"N6UA, has 1 onboard and fuel is one plus one fife."

🎧 Now, say it out loud:

Explanation: 38 liters / 30.3 liters per hour = 1.25 hours or 1 hour and 15 minutes.

5. The approach controller tells you the weather at the airport is sky clear, visibility 10 miles, surface winds are calm and the altimeter is 30.01. He tells you Evansville Regional is currently landing and departing Runway 18, which is 6,286 feet long. The controller informs you that he can get authorization to let you land straight-in on Runway 36 if you would prefer. You will be approaching the airport from the south. Given your situation, would you prefer Runway 18 or Runway 36?

Circle your answer:

Runway 18. Runway 36.

↓↓ANSWER↓↓

Runway 36 would be the preferred answer.

Explanation. The winds are calm, so they do not influence your choice of runway. Since your approach will conveniently align you with that runway. If you selected Runway 18, you would have to travel to the north end of the airport to land, adding extra flying time. With indications of fire, you need to get on the ground as soon as possible.

6. What service, relevant to your emergency, would you ask ATC to have standing by for your landing?

_____

_____

↓↓**ANSWER**↓↓

You would request to have the airport fire department meet your aircraft after landing.

Explanation: Air traffic controllers are sharp enough to anticipate the need for airport fire and rescue for any pilot who says he has indications of fire on board. It is still a good idea to verify this coordination has taken place.

7. Considering your emergency, would you anticipate stopping on the runway after landing, or taxiing clear of the runway after landing?

Circle the correct answer:

Stop on the runway.   Taxi clear.

↓↓**ANSWER**↓↓

Stop on the runway.

Explanation: This is a judgment call. Considering you have what appears to be a worsening fire, probably in the engine, taxiing after landing would not be a good idea. Personally, I would not only shut down on the runway, I would also evacuate the airplane after shutting down.

8. Write the radio call you would make to ATC indicating your intentions after landing:

_____

_____

↓↓**ANSWER**↓↓

"N6UA will be stopping on the runway and shutting down (or, evacuating)."

Now, say it out loud:

9. Let's change this scenario just a little bit. You are in the same setup: smoke, rough running engine, same fuel remaining, and you are flying solo. This time, you are carrying some flammable chemicals (three 32-ounce bottles of propane) in the cargo area of your aircraft. Assume you have already made your emergency declaration with ATC and passed along the requested information. Write what else you would add to alert ATC about the chemicals:

_____

_____

↓↓ANSWER↓↓

"Be advised, N6UA is carrying tree 32-ounce bottles of propane in the cargo compartment."

🎧 Now, say it out loud:

Explanation: The AIM (6-3-2 3. k. Obtaining Emergency Assistance) says to include any other "useful information" in your message. This information would be very helpful to the airport fire and rescue service when they respond to your emergency.

Evansville Approach replies, "N6UA, I copy tree 32-ounce bottles of propane in the cargo compartment. I'll pass that information to the fire chief."

10. Now, let's say, as you proceed inbound under an emergency for smoke and a rough-running engine, the smoke stops and the engine smoothes out to a normal level of operation. Would you cancel your emergency with ATC?

Circle the correct answer:

Yes. No. Maybe.

↓↓ANSWER↓↓

No.

Explanation: This is a judgment call. There is no absolutely correct answer. I personally would retain my emergency status with ATC because I could not tell with absolute certainty that the fire is completely out or that it will not start up again at any moment. Additionally, I don't know how much engine damage has occurred. A damaged engine that is running well now may not run well as I make power changes during my approach and landing. If you cancel your emergency status, you will no longer receive priority to land, and ATC will cancel fire and rescue service for your aircraft.

11. This time, as you are inbound to Evansville Regional, not only does the smoke increase in the cockpit, but you can see flames shooting out of the engine compartment. The engine sounds like it might quit at any moment. You are still 10 miles from the Evansville Airport. You look down and see an east-west runway, only a 1/2 mile off your left wing, that looks like it is long enough to land on. What would you do in this

situation and what would you say to ATC?

_____

_____

_____

↓↓ANSWER↓↓

You would choose to land on the nearest suitable airport, which, in this case is the airport 1/2 mile to your left. You would advise ATC about the change in plan.

Note: In an emergency tell ATC what you plan to do. Don't ask. As pilot-in-command during an emergency, you are free to do whatever is necessary to ensure safety. This includes ignoring any regulation that stands between you and a safe outcome to your flight. (ADD CFR.)

As always, maintain aircraft control first, navigate second, and advise ATC only when time and conditions permit. Never sacrifice aircraft control or safe navigation while focusing on radio communication.

Fog

Your call sign is Skylane 571LS. You started a VFR cross-country flight across New England on what was supposed to be a nice autumn day. As you fly north on V-91, in Western Vermont, the scattered layer of clouds above you becomes broken. Soon, the broken layer fills in until it is an overcast layer of clouds. There is no problem though, because there is still plenty of vertical space under the overcast layer to allow you to continue VFR.

As you continue, you notice the outside air temperature is dropping and the visibility is starting to decrease. The visibility goes from 10 miles to 5 miles. In a few more minutes, the visibility has dropped to 4 miles. You fly through patches where the visibility has decreased to 3 miles in fog. Certain that if you continue north, the visibility will go below 3 miles, you decide to turn around.

1. As you head south, you notice the visibility is not improving as you had expected. Concerned that you might get trapped at any minute in weather that is less than VFR, you give Boston Center a call and receive the reply, "Radar contact" from ATC. Write what you would say to the controller in Boston Center for help finding your way out of the marginal VFR weather:

_____

_____

Any statement that gets the following intent across is correct: "Skylane 571LS needs to land at the nearest airport reporting VFR conditions." (AIM 6-2-1 Radar Service for VFR Aircraft in Difficulty.)

 Now, say it out loud:

Explanation: ATC cannot give vectors to avoid low visibility. All ATC can do with regards to visibility is tell you about general areas of VFR weather shown on a surface weather depiction map or about airports reporting VFR weather. Surface depiction maps are updated only once every 3 hours and only show broad areas of weather conditions. Airport weather stations report at least once per hour, and more frequently when weather conditions are changing. ATC will be able to give you the most accurate and timely weather information at airports in your area. ATC may also be able to get reports from other pilots in your area about inflight weather conditions.

2. Boston Center says, "Skylane 1LS, Rutland Regional Airport is tree zero miles southeast of your current position. The current weather for Rutland is 3,500 overcast, visibility 5 miles. Temperature 14, dewpoint 12. Winds are 020 at 8 knots. The Rutland altimeter is 29.87. The longest runway at Rutland is Runway 1 with 5,000 feet available. They have an FBO on the field. Would you like vectors to Rutland?"

Write your reply to Boston Center:

_____

_____

"Skylane 1LS, affirmative."

 Now, say it out loud:

Boston Center says, "Skylane 571LS, roger. Turn right heading one two zero. Maintain VFR and advise me of any altitude changes."

ATC can give you general information about precipitation levels in your area. For example, an enroute controller might say, "Skylane 571LS, light to moderate to extreme precipitation beginning at your 12 o'clock and 10 miles and continuing for the next 20 miles." ATC cannot pinpoint precipitation with a level of accuracy that would allow precise vectoring around precipitation.

The very rare exception to this rule occurs at TRACONs at some of the nation's busiest airports. Some approach control facilities have Doppler radar integrated into their air traffic control displays. ATC will respond to your request to steer away from bad weather. Let's practice.

3. Your call sign remains Skylane 571LS, but now you are flying in South Florida. It's late afternoon and widely scattered thunderstorms are popping up in your area. Just as you spot a thunderstorm in your path, Miami Center says, "Skylane 571LS, an area of moderate to extreme precipitation extending from your 11 to 1 o'clock and one fife miles extends approximately one zero miles to the southeast." Write your reply to Miami Center, indicating you would like to deviate around the weather:

_____

_____

↓↓**ANSWER** ↓↓

"Skylane 571LS, copies. We'll deviate around that weather to the [general direction, such as north or west]."

Now, say it out loud:

Miami says, "Skylane 571LS, roger. Maintain VFR and keep me advised."

Medical Emergencies

New day, new airplane. You are flying a Cherokee 6, call sign Piper 323YA, with 4 passengers from Cape May, New Jersey to York, Pennsylvania. You are in radar contact with Washington Center for VFR flight following as you cross the Delaware River north of Dover, Delaware. As you approach the western shore of the river, you hear a loud moan from the back seat of your passenger cabin. Then, the person sitting in the right rear seat yells, "I think Joe is having a heart attack!"

You have the Cherokee's autopilot on, so you quickly turn around and look back. Sure enough, Joe Jergens, approximate age mid-50s, sitting in the left rear seat, is grimacing as he clutches his chest. He is extremely pale, gasping for air, and sweating heavily.

1. No one on your airplane has any medical experience. Write the radio call you would make to Washington Center:

_____

_____

↓↓**ANSWER** ↓↓

"Piper 323YA is declaring a medical emergency. I have a passenger who may be having a heart attack."

191

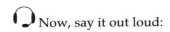Now, say it out loud:

Explanation: Earlier, in the section on making initial contact with an enroute center, I presented a situation in which you had smoke in the cockpit (p. 57). In that situation, I said you should go no further than stating you have an emergency when making initial contact with ATC.

In the medical emergency presented here, you are already in contact with Washington Center. The controller knows who you are and where you are. You can be more specific in your emergency declaration. A simple statement, such as, "I have a passenger who may be having a heart attack," is enough to get started. Avoid the temptation to give a long description in one radio transmission.

2. Washington Center says, "Piper 3YA, copy your medical emergency. Let me see if I can get you a PPR to land at Dover Air Force Base at your 8 o'clock and 25 miles. When you have time, can you give me the passenger's first and last name and his approximate age?" (PPR stands for Prior Permission Required. It is a reservation to land at a military airport. Dover Air Force Base normally requires a PPR made 72 hours in advance of arrival.) Write your reply to Washington Center:

_____

_____

↓↓ANSWER↓↓

"Piper 3YA, the passenger's name is Joe Jergens, approximate age mid-50s."

Now, say it out loud:

3. Washington Center says, "Piper 3YA, I copy. Unfortunately Dover will not authorize a PPR for you due to an exercise they are running at the base. I've got Delaware Airpark at your 10 o'clock and 20 miles with 3,200 feet of runway available and limited services. The nearest hospital to that airport is in the city of Dover, approximately 20 miles away. I also have Millville Municipal at your 4 o'clock and 20 miles with 6,000 feet of runway. The nearest hospital to Millville is in town, 5 miles away. Say your intentions." (You would choose Millville in this case due to the proximity of the hospital.) Write your reply to Washington Center:

_____

_____

↓↓ANSWER↓↓

"Piper 3YA will take a vector to Millville."

Now, say it out loud:

4. Washington Center says, "Piper 3YA, for vectors to Millville, turn right heading zero niner zero. We are calling ahead now to have paramedics meet your airplane on arrival. When you have time, say the number of people on board and fuel remaining. (Your fuel remaining is 2 hours.) Write your reply to Washington Center:

↓↓**ANSWER** ↓↓

"Piper 3YA right, heading zero niner zero. We have 5 people on board. Fuel on board is 2 hours."

Now, say it out loud:

5. Washington Center says, "Piper 3YA, Millville is an uncontrolled airport. The traffic advisory frequency is 123.65. When you're ready to copy, I have the latest weather and landing information for Millville." You are ready to copy. Write your reply to Washington Center:

↓↓**ANSWER** ↓↓

"Piper 3YA is ready to copy."

Now, say it out loud:

6. Washington Center says, "Millville is reporting fife thousand fife hundred scattered. Visibility is one zero. Temperature one eight. Dewpoint one two. The wind is zero niner zero at tree. Altimeter tree zero two zero. Millville is landing and departing Runway One Zero. Traffic pattern altitude is one thousand feet. I'm not showing any NOTAMs for that airport." Write your reply to Washington Center:

↓↓**ANSWER** ↓↓

"Piper 3YA, altimeter tree zero two zero."

Now, say it out loud:

193

7. Washington Center says, "Piper 3YA, paramedics are on the way. The airport is at your 12 o'clock and one fife miles and you are almost lined up with Runway 10. Report the airport in sight." (You see the airport and the runway.) Write your reply to Washington Center:

_____

↓↓**ANSWER**↓↓

"Piper 3YA has the airport in sight."

🎧 Now, say it out loud:

Washington Center says, "Piper 3YA, I'm told paramedics are already at the airport and standing by on the ramp on the north side of the airport. Switch over to Millville's traffic advisory frequency 123.65. Good luck."

8. When you switch to Millville's CTAF, what key word would you include with your call sign during your position reports to Millville traffic?

_____ .

↓↓**ANSWER**↓↓

"Emergency."

Explanation: Although not guaranteed, using the word "emergency" in your calls to traffic at the airport should tell other pilots in the airport pattern to yield to your aircraft. Don't assume this will be the case however. Clear for traffic and fit into the traffic flow as necessary.

9. Given your emergency and your present position, would you enter the pattern via a midfield downwind entry for Runway 10, or would you continue directly toward a straight-in final approach for Runway 10?

Circle your answer:

Midfield downwind entry.   Straight-in final approach.

↓↓**ANSWER**↓↓

Straight-in final approach.

Explanation: In any emergency, the shortest path to the runway is almost always the correct choice.

Lost: A Potential Emergency

Being lost is not an emergency until you reach a point where you are lost and getting low on fuel. I'll have more about this in a few minutes. For now, let's get lost.

You are flying your Cherokee 6, call sign Piper 323YA, 500 feet above the ground over forested area in central South Carolina. You are taking great care not to fly closer than 500 feet to any person or obstacle on the ground, per regulations. Unfortunately, as you continue your low-level VFR flight on a hot summer day, the sky is extremely hazy. Although the visibility is well within VFR limits, you feel like you are flying in a milk bowl.

With miles and miles of forest in every direction, it is very had to pinpoint where you are on your sectional map. Every logging road looks like every other logging road and there is no distinguishing terrain or manmade feature to help you stay oriented. After flying like this for 30 minutes, you realize you are lost.

Thinking you might be somewhere between Florence and Sumter, South Carolina, you tune the Florence VORTAC into your navigation radio. When you reach to spin the VOR compass dial, you see an off flag in the VOR display instrument. The DME indicator shows only dashed lines in its face.

1. Next, you try the McEntire VORTAC, which you believe is to your west. You get an off flag for McEntire and dash marks in the DME indicator. You must be either out of range or below a suitable altitude to receive either VORTAC. What is the first thing you should do to help correct your situation?

_____

_____

↓↓ANSWER↓↓

Climb to a higher altitude. (There is an extensive discussion in *Radio Mastery for VFR Aircraft* on what to do after becoming lost.)

You try climbing, but you still cannot receive either VORTAC. You cannot see any further at this altitude either. You are still lost.

2. ATC could help. Where could you look to find an appropriate frequency to contact an air traffic control tower or an approach control facility?

_____

↓↓ANSWER↓↓

On a sectional chart, or enroute chart for the area in which you are flying.

3. You dial in the frequency for Florence Tower in your number one communication radio. Write what you would say to make initial contact with Florence Tower:

_____

_____

↓↓**ANSWER**↓↓

"Florence Tower, Piper 323YA."

🎧 Now, say it out loud:

Explanation: There is no point in saying anything more until you connect with Florence Tower.

4. The controller in Florence Tower comes through weak and unreadable. You try to reach Sumter Approach Control but get the same unusable result. What other person or facility can you try to reach by radio? (Here, I'm asking for types of facilities or people, not specific names.)

_____.

_____.

_____.

↓↓**ANSWER**↓↓

An air route traffic control center (ARTCC).

A flight service station (FSS).

Any pilot on any frequency who can relay your situation to ATC.

5. Where can you find a frequency for an enroute control center (ARTCC)?

_____

↓↓**ANSWER**↓↓

On an enroute low chart.

6. If you cannot find a workable frequency to contact ATC, what single, universal frequency could you use to contact ATC, FSS or another pilot?

_____

↓↓**ANSWER**↓↓

121.5

7. What 2-way radio frequency, used by many flight service locations in the U.S., could you use to try to contact an FSS?

↓↓**ANSWER**↓↓

122.2

8. Let's say you find a frequency in which both ATC and other pilots are coming through loud and clear. What code words could you use to command radio silence, allowing you to immediately state your non-emergency problem?

_____

↓↓**ANSWER**↓↓

Pan Pan Pan. (AIM 6-3-1 c. and d. Distress and Urgency Communications.)

9. You have managed to reach Jacksonville (Jax) Center on 127.95. The controller says, "Piper 323YA, say the nature of your problem." Write your reply to Jax Center:

_____

↓↓**ANSWER**↓↓

"Skylane Piper 323YA is lost."

🎧 Now, say it out loud:

Explanation: I know this is a difficult thing to admit on the radio. The sooner you say it, the quicker ATC will be able to solve your problem. Do not waste time and fuel skipping around the problem. Say you are lost, pure and simple.

10. Jax Center says, "Piper 323YA, squawk 5362 and ident." Write your reply to Jax Center:

_____

_____

↓↓ANSWER↓↓

"Piper 323YA, 5362 with an ident."

🎧 Now, say it out loud:

11. Jax Center says, "Piper 323YA, Charleston altimeter 29.95. Say your altitude." (You are currently at 3,500 feet MSL.) Write your reply to Jax Center:

_____

_____

↓↓ANSWER↓↓

"Piper 323YA, 29.95. We are at tree thousand, fife hundred."

🎧 Now, say it out loud:

Jax Center says, "Piper 323YA, I'm not picking you up. Try tuning the Vance VOR on 110.4. Are you DME equipped?" You tell Jax Center you have DME on board. When you tune the Vance VORTAC, you see the same thing you did for the other VORTACs: an off flag in the VOR instrument face and dashes in the DME indicator. You relay this information to Jax Center.

Jax Center says, "Piper 323YA, I would tell you to climb higher but there are several MOAs in my airspace and I don't want you climbing into those. Try the Allendale VOR on 116.7. It does not have DME, but maybe we can locate you on a radial for Allendale." You acknowledge this transmission and tune in Allendale.

12. This time, you are able to receive the VOR. You spin the dial on the VOR instrument and center the needle with a "From" indication on the 240-degree radial. Write your radio call to Jax Center:

_____

_____

↓↓ANSWER↓↓

"Piper 323YA is on the Allendale two four zero degree radial."

Now, say it out loud:

Jax Center says, "Piper 323YA, copy the 240-degree radial off Allendale. That would put you in another sector for Jax Center. Standby." You wait about 15 seconds, and then the controller says, "Piper 323YA, my counterpart on the other side of the room says he has your airplane in radar contact, two zero miles southwest of the Allendale VOR. Contact Jax Center now on 132.5 and he'll get you back on course to wherever you want to go."

New day, same airplane, same situation, with one exception. Your right wing fuel tank is empty and your left wing fuel tank's indicator is bouncing between 1/4 and 1/2. By the time you realize you are lost over the forests of South Carolina, you calculate you have only 30 to 40 minutes of fuel remaining.

As before, you try tuning a couple of VORTACs with no success. As before, you try reaching Florence Tower and Sumter Approach with no success. Your fuel indicator is now bouncing around the 1/4 mark. Place a check mark next to the correct answer. At this point, would you:

1. _____ Continue trying to get in touch with ATC.

2. _____ Find any suitable airport or suitable landing surface and land as soon as possible.

↓↓ANSWER↓↓

Answer 2.

Explanation: Do you really need an explanation as to why this is the best course of action? I didn't think so.

You scan the ground below and see a grass landing strip, next to a farm, which appears to be at least 1,500 feet long. (Your airplane can make a short-field landing or takeoff in 900 feet.) You also see a small town 3 miles off your left wing. If that town is Sylvania, your sectional shows there is an airport with paved runways. The chart shows the longest runway is 5,000 feet long. You cannot see the paved airport due to the low visibility and the fact your chart shows it about 5 miles south of town. You are also not sure that town is Sylvania because you are not sure of your present position.

Place a check mark next to the correct answer:

14. You would:

     1. _____ Try to contact ATC to get a fix on your position and help you identify the town.

     2. _____ Fly south 10 miles to try and find the airport with the paved runways.

     3. _____ Land on the grass strip next to the farm.

↓↓ANSWER↓↓

Answer 3.

Explanation: Forget about contacting ATC. ATC cannot put fuel back in your tank and the process of trying to get in contact with ATC will take more time than you have. Spending additional time trying to find an airport when you aren't even sure of your location is also a bad idea. The grass strip you can see is a suitable airport. Land there.

Final

There are some emergencies that are so desperate that it is strongly recommended you begin your transmission with the word "Mayday" spoken 3 times: "Mayday, mayday, mayday."

1. List some emergencies that might prompt you to use "Mayday."

Note: The AIM tells you to use "Mayday" for all distress situations. (AIM 6-3-1 Distress and Urgency Communications.) You are never wrong to use "Mayday" in any emergency situation. Most pilots reserve the word for dire circumstances.

_____

_____

_____

_____

_____

↓↓ANSWER↓↓

The following list does not cover every situation in which it might be appropriate to say "Mayday."

-Loss of all aircraft engines with no possibility of an engine restart.

-Uncontrollable fire inside the aircraft fuselage.

-Loss, or imminent loss of aircraft control.

Note: Includes insufficient power to remain aloft; or, unresponsive aircraft control surfaces.

-Pilot incapacitation with no pilot backup onboard, such as a second pilot or an autopilot.

Note: Incapacitation may include spatial disorientation, health issues, or loss of consciousness. The Mayday call may have to be made by a passenger.

-An act of terrorism or other onboard violence that threatens life or aircraft control.

2. This last question on emergencies does not specifically address radio procedure. It is more general in nature, and, it does relate to what you can say on the radio. What does Part 91 of the consolidated federal regulations allow you to do, as pilot-in-command, in the event of an emergency?

_____

_____

↓↓ANSWER↓↓

"In an in-flight emergency requiring immediate action, the pilot in command may deviate from any rule of this part to the extent required to meet that emergency." (CFR 91.3 (b).)

Think Like a Controller

You are working the approach controller position for the north sector of the Little Rock TRACON. A pilot checks in on your frequency saying, "Little Rock Approach, Diamond 3361F, twenty-fife miles north of Little Rock, VFR with a medical emergency." At the same time, a radar target 5 miles north of the edge of your airspace appears, showing the emergency code 7-7-0-0. You assign a transponder code to the aircraft and the emergency squawk changes to a normal radar datablock for the aircraft.

1. What specific information do you need to obtain from the pilot of this emergency aircraft?

_____

_____

_____

_____

_____

↓↓ANSWER↓↓

(Note: The order of information is not important.)

Pilot's intentions.

Type of medical problem.

Name and approximate age of the person with the medical problem.

Number of people on board.

Fuel remaining.

2. Having established the pilot wants to land at Little Rock International Airport, you would:

(Place a check mark next to the correct answer.)

1. _____ Place this airplane in the normal sequence for landing at Little Rock.

2. _____ Move other aircraft out of this airplane's path and allow the pilot to fly direct to a short final approach at Little Rock.

↓↓ANSWER↓↓

Answer 2.

3. You are now the local controller (Tower) at Little Rock International Airport. One of your approach controllers has just called you on the landline to say Diamond 3361F is approximately 7 minutes from landing at your airport. Who would you notify to meet the emergency aircraft after it lands?

_____.

↓↓**ANSWER**↓↓

Paramedics / Ambulance

4. Would you expect this emergency aircraft to stop on the runway, shutting down operations for that runway for a period of time, or would you expect the aircraft to taxi clear of the runway after landing?

Circle the correct answer:

Stop on the runway.   Taxi clear of the runway.

↓↓**ANSWER**↓↓

Taxi clear of the runway.

Note: You would anticipate telling the pilot to taxi to a place where paramedics could meet the airplane.

5. New day, new situation. You are still on duty in Little Rock Tower. This time, Approach says he has an emergency aircraft inbound to your airport. The nature of his emergency is smoke in the cockpit and the smoke is intensifying. Approach tells you the pilot is so busy coping with his emergency that the controller has not been able to determine what the pilot intends to do after landing. Would you expect the pilot of this aircraft to:

Circle the correct answer:

Stop on the runway.   Taxi clear of the runway.

↓↓**ANSWER**↓↓

Stop on the runway.

Note: This is a vital bit of information because if the pilot stops on the runway, it will suspend operations on that runway until the aircraft can be removed.

Flying Into or Over Big Airports. Plus, Making Quick Work of TRSAs.

The largest, busiest airports in the United States are surrounded by Class Bravo airspace. We are talking about airports such as Chicago's O'Hare, Los Angeles' LAX, New York's LaGuardia and Kennedy, and Atlanta's Hartsfield-Jackson, for example. Class B is usually restricted to IFR traffic with reservations to land at the airport inside the airspace. It is extremely rare for ATC to allow VFR traffic to fly through Class B airspace, let alone land at the airport inside.

Class Bravo is usually so filled with a steady stream of IFR arrivals and departures that ATC does not have time to handle the additional load created by VFR traffic transiting the airspace. There are exceptions, however.

Certain Class Bravo structures have built-in VFR transition routes that allow pilots to cross over or fly near the primary airport without having to fly miles out of the way to circle around the airspace. Presently the Class B airspace exceptions to the rule are Seattle, Washington; Phoenix, Arizona; Los Angeles, California; and New York City, New York. As a pilot flying under VFR, you may position your aircraft at any of the entrance points around these Class Bravo structures and work with ATC to fly the transition route past busy airports. Let's try some examples, beginning in Los Angeles.

Your call sign is Cirrus 9241B. You are proceeding northwest on V-23 at 6,500 MSL. You have just passed over the John Wayne Orange County Airport. Your altitude puts you above the Class C airspace surrounding the airport. You are approaching the charted visual landmark labeled Mile Square Park, which is at your 2 o'clock position and 3 miles. This landmark lies exactly on the edge of the Class Bravo airspace surrounding LAX. (Refer to the Los Angeles Terminal Area Chart segment, below.)

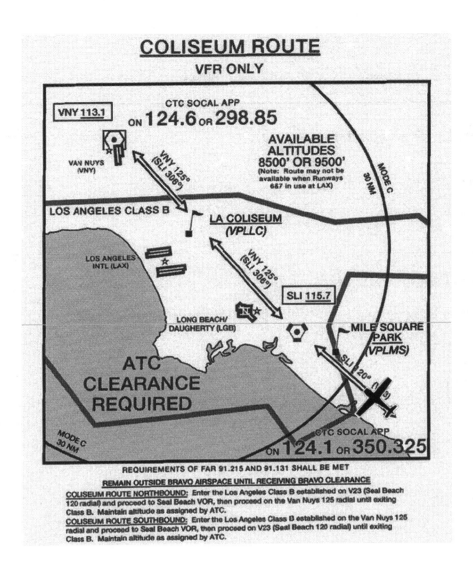

COLISEUM ROUTE

VFR ONLY

CTC SOCAL APP
ON **124.6** OR **298.85**

VNY 113.1

VAN NUYS (VNY)

AVAILABLE ALTITUDES
8500' OR 9500'
(Note: Route may not be available when Runways 6&7 in use at LAX)

VNY 125° (SLI 306°)

MODE C 30 NM

LOS ANGELES CLASS B

LA COLISEUM (VPLLC)

LOS ANGELES INTL (LAX)

VNY 125° (SLI 306°)

SLI 115.7

LONG BEACH/ DAUGHERTY (LGB)

MILE SQUARE PARK (VPLMS)

ATC CLEARANCE REQUIRED

SLI 120° (V-23)

MODE C 30 NM

CTC SOCAL APP
ON **124.1** OR **350.325**

REQUIREMENTS OF FAR 91.215 AND 91.131 SHALL BE MET
REMAIN OUTSIDE BRAVO AIRSPACE UNTIL RECEIVING BRAVO CLEARANCE
COLISEUM ROUTE NORTHBOUND: Enter the Los Angeles Class B established on V23 (Seal Beach 120 radial) and proceed to Seal Beach VOR, then proceed on the Van Nuys 125 radial until exiting Class B. Maintain altitude as assigned by ATC.
COLISEUM ROUTE SOUTHBOUND: Enter the Los Angeles Class B established on the Van Nuys 125 radial and proceed to Seal Beach VOR, then proceed on V23 (Seal Beach 120 radial) until exiting Class B. Maintain altitude as assigned by ATC.

1. Are you allowed to proceed past Mile Square Park, at your current altitude, without ATC's permission?

Circle your answer:

    Yes. No. Maybe.

↓↓ANSWER↓↓

    No.

    Explanation: Flying past Mile Square Park will put your aircraft inside Class B airspace. You may not do this without ATC's permission. (AIM 3-2-3 d. 2. (a) Class Bravo VFR Flights.)

2. You decide to contact SoCal Approach (Southern California Approach) as you reach a point on V-23 abeam Mile Square Park. Your intention is to proceed on the Coliseum Route to transition the Class B. Write the radio call you would make to SoCal Approach:

_____

_____

═══

"SoCal Approach, Cirrus 9241B, approaching Mile Square Park, 6,500, for the Coliseum Route."

🎧 Now, say it out loud:

3. SoCal Approach says, "Cirrus 9241B, SoCal Approach, standby. Break, break, Twin Cessna 3RZ, I show you clear of the Class Bravo. Squawk 1200 and frequency change approved." At this point, having made radio contact with SoCal Approach, may you enter Class Bravo airspace?

Circle your answer:

Yes. No. Maybe.

═══

No.

Explanation: ATC must specifically say, "Cleared to enter Class Bravo airspace," before you may enter. (AIM 3-2-3 d. 2. (a) Class Bravo VFR Flights.)

4. SoCal Approach says, "Cirrus 9248B, squawk 0612 and ident. Remain clear of the Class Bravo." Write your reply to SoCal Approach:

_____

_____

═══

"Cirrus 9248, 0612 and ident and we'll remain clear of the Class Bravo."

🎧 Now, say it out loud:

5. SoCal Approach says, "Cirrus 48B, radar contact, 6,500 over Mile Square Park. Climb and maintain 8,500 east of Mile Square Park." Write your reply to SoCal Approach:

_____

_____

↓↓**ANSWER** ↓↓

" Cirrus 48B, climb and maintain 8,500 east of Mile Square Park."

Now, say it out loud:

6. SoCal Approach says, "Cirrus 48B, after passing 7,000 you're cleared to enter the Class Bravo and fly the Coliseum Route." Write your readback:

_____

_____

↓↓**ANSWER** ↓↓

"Cirrus 48B, passing 7,000 cleared to enter the Class Bravo and fly the Coliseum Route."

Now, say it out loud:

7. Shortly after you pass the Los Angeles Coliseum on V-23, SoCal Approach says, "Cirrus 48B, I show you exiting the Class Bravo. Squawk 1200 and frequency change approved." Write your reply to SoCal Approach:

_____

_____

↓↓**ANSWER** ↓↓

"Cirrus 48B, squawking 1200 and switching."

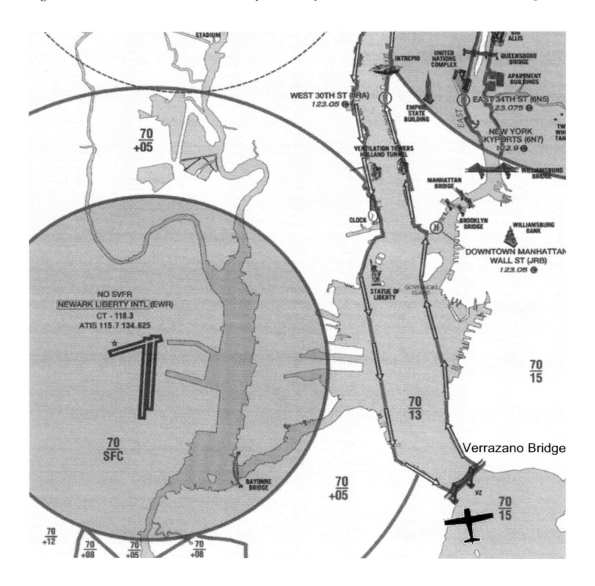

Now, say it out loud:

New day, new airplane. You are flying a Pitts S-2C northbound on the edge of the Jersey Shore, approaching the Verrazano Bridge. (See chart below.) Your call sign is Pitts 7821G. You are at an altitude of 1,500 feet MSL. You would like to transition through New York's Class Bravo airspace to continue north towards Newburg, New York (north of New York City). The Skyline Route would work best for this plan.

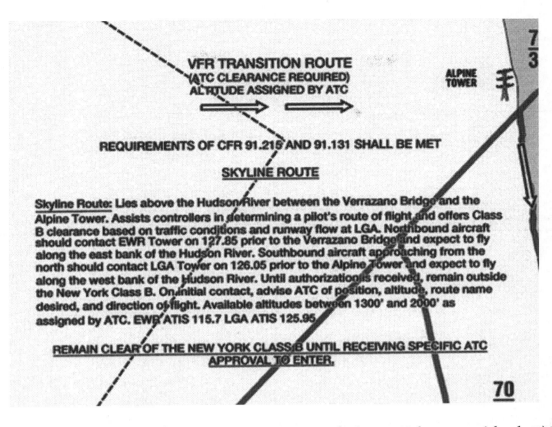

VFR TRANSITION ROUTE
(ATC CLEARANCE REQUIRED)
ALTITUDE ASSIGNED BY ATC

REQUIREMENTS OF CFR 91.215 AND 91.131 SHALL BE MET

SKYLINE ROUTE

Skyline Route: Lies above the Hudson River between the Verrazano Bridge and the Alpine Tower. Assists controllers in determining a pilot's route of flight and offers Class B clearance based on traffic conditions and runway flow at LGA. Northbound aircraft should contact EWR Tower on 127.85 prior to the Verrazano Bridge and expect to fly along the east bank of the Hudson River. Southbound aircraft approaching from the north should contact LGA Tower on 126.05 prior to the Alpine Tower and expect to fly along the west bank of the Hudson River. Until authorization is received, remain outside the New York Class B. On initial contact, advise ATC of position, altitude, route name desired, and direction of flight. Available altitudes between 1300' and 2000' as assigned by ATC. EWR ATIS 115.7 LGA ATIS 125.95.

REMAIN CLEAR OF THE NEW YORK CLASS B UNTIL RECEIVING SPECIFIC ATC APPROVAL TO ENTER.

8. As you approach the Verrazano Bridge (the bridge depicted in the bottom right corner of the chart) in New York Harbor, what frequency would you tune in your communication radio to contact ATC? (See chart notes, above.)

_____.

↓↓ANSWER↓↓

127.85

9. Write the radio call you would make to ATC to establish initial contact:

_____

_____

↓↓ANSWER↓↓

"Newark Tower, Pitts 7821G, south of the Verazzano Bridge, 1,500, for the Skyline Route."

🎧 Now, say it out loud:

10. The controller in Newark Tower says, "Pitts 7821G, squawk 0340 and remain clear of the Class Bravo." Write your reply to Newark Tower:

_____

↓↓**ANSWER**↓↓

"Pitts 7821G, 0340 and we'll remain clear of the Class Bravo."

🎧 Now, say it out loud:

11. The controller in Newark Tower says, "Pitts 21G, radar contact. You're cleared to enter the Class Bravo. Maintain VFR at 2,000 and proceed north on the Skyline Route." Write your reply to Newark Tower:

_____

_____

↓↓**ANSWER**↓↓

"Pitts 21G, cleared to enter the Class Bravo, VFR at 2,000. We'll proceed north on the Skyline Route."

🎧 Now, say it out loud:

Newark Tower says, "Pitts 21G, report passing the Intrepid." You acknowledge this radio call and note the Intrepid is a charted reporting point over the aircraft carrier exhibit on the Hudson River.

12. After several minutes, you are about to pass over the Intrepid. Write the radio call you would make to Newark Tower:

_____

↓↓**ANSWER**↓↓

"Pitts 21G is passing the Intrepid."

Now, say it out loud:

Newark Tower says, "Pitts 21G, traffic is a helicopter at 500 southbound along the river at your 11 o'clock and 3 miles. Report passing the Alpine Tower." (See the chart below depicting the Alpine Tower.) You see the helicopter ahead and below you.

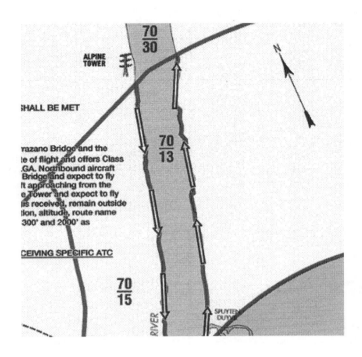

13. Write your reply to Newark Tower:

_____

_____

_____

↓↓**ANSWER** ↓↓

"Pitts 21G has the helicopter in sight. We'll report passing the Alpine Tower."

Now, say it out loud:

14. As the Alpine Tower passes off your left wing, you make a position report to Newark Tower. Write that radio call:

_____

_____

"Pitts 21G, passing the Alpine Tower."

🎧 Now, say it out loud:

15. Newark Tower says, "Pitts 21G, you're exiting the Class Bravo. Resume VFR altitudes and squawk 1200. Frequency change approved." Write your reply to Newark Tower:

_____

_____

"Pitts 21G, resuming VFR altitudes. Squawking 1200 and switching."

🎧 Now, say it out loud:

While it is highly unlikely you will get permission to cross through Class Bravo airspace while VFR at any location that does not have VFR transition routes, you might prove the exception to the rule. Let's cover a few important points you will need to know before penetrating Class Bravo airspace and *not* on a VFR transition route.

16. While inside Class B, what is the minimum separation you must maintain from clouds?

_____

Clear of clouds. (CFR 91.155)

17. While inside Class B, what is the minimum inflight visibility you must maintain?

_____

↓↓**ANSWER**↓↓

3 statute miles. (CFR 91.155)

18. If a heading or altitude assignment by ATC would cause you to violate VFR cloud clearance minimums, what are you required to do?

_____

↓↓**ANSWER**↓↓

Request an amended clearance from ATC that allows you to remain VFR. (AIM 5-5-6 a. 3. Radar Vectors.)

19. Check which flight parameters ATC may include in a clearance while you are inside Class B airspace:

_____ Heading

_____ Altitude

_____ Airspeed

_____ Vertical speed

↓↓**ANSWER**↓↓

All of the above may be included in a clearance from ATC. (AIM 3-2-3 2. e. Class Bravo VFR Flights.)

213

20. While in Class B airspace, and not in a VFR transition corridor, ATC will mostly like assign:

(Circle the correct answer.)

Whole altitudes, eg. 3,000; 4,000; 9,000; etc. / VFR hemispheric altitudes, eg. 3,500; 4,500; 9,500.

↓↓ANSWER↓↓

Whole altitudes. (AIM 3-2-3 2. e. 4. Class Bravo VFR Flights.)

Example: "Cessna 9130D, descend and maintain 4,000."

21. If ATC adds, "Best rate to 4,000," in your words, what does the controller want you to do?

_____

_____

↓↓ANSWER↓↓

Descend at the maximum rate of descent your aircraft is capable of in its current configuration.

Explanation: The AIM Pilot/Controller Glossary uses the term "expedite" here: "Expedite climb/descent normally indicates to a pilot that the approximate best rate of climb/descent should be used without requiring an exceptional change in aircraft handling characteristics." Air traffic controllers have extracted the words "best rate" from this definition to tell pilots to climb or descend quickly.

22. If you are maintaining your best rate of descent per ATC's direction, what should you do during the last 1,000 of climb or descent before your assigned altitude?

_____

_____

↓↓ANSWER↓↓

Reduce your rate of descent to 1,500 feet per minute or less.

Explanation: This is a strongly recommended technique to prevent overshooting your assigned level-off altitude.

23. You are landing at a large international airport inside Class B airspace. ATC has told you that a Boeing 747 is 5 miles behind you on final approach with 70 knots of overtaking airspeed. Should you fly:

(Place a check mark next to the correct answer.)

1. _____ Cruise airspeed until crossing the threshold of the runway, then slow to lower flaps and land.

2. _____ Fly your normal final approach, slowing to final approach airspeed and landing flaps as you would in any other circumstance.

↓↓ANSWER↓↓

Answer 2.

Explanation: Do not let ATC's sense of urgency encourage you to fly a fast, unstable approach and landing. For a more extensive discussion of why this is important, read the section on operations at busy airports in *Radio Mastery for VFR Pilots*, Chapter 16.

24. As you touch down at a big international airport, the tower controller says, "Traffic is a Boeing Triple-7 on a 2-mile final. Make the first right turn off the runway." Just prior to reaching the first right turn, your groundspeed is still very high. If you attempt to make the turn as directed, you might lock the brakes and skid or blow a tire. What should you say to the tower controller?

_____

_____

↓↓ANSWER↓↓

Your call sign, plus "Unable the first right turnoff."

🎧 Now, say it out loud:

25. Tower says to the Boeing 777, "I might have to send you around if the Cessna on landing roll doesn't make the first turnoff." You are the Cessna that Tower is talking about. Would that make you attempt to try the first right turn, even if your groundspeed was still very high?

Circle the correct answer:

Yes. No. Maybe.

↓↓**ANSWER**↓↓

No.

Explanation: We have beaten this subject to death. Enough said.

26. You are departing from an airport inside Class Bravo. Departure Control has assigned an altitude of 4,000. You reach this altitude and level off. As you exit the Class Bravo airspace, Departure Control says, "You are exiting the Class Bravo. Resume VFR altitudes." What does Departure Control expect you to do with regard to altitude?

_____

_____

↓↓**ANSWER**↓↓

Climb or descend to an appropriate VFR cruising altitude (such as 4,500 or 3,500). (AIM 3-2-3 2. e. 4. Class Bravo VFR Flights.)

A Very Brief Discussion of Terminal Radar Services Areas (TRSA)

1. A TRSA most closely resembles which other class of airspace in *physical layout*?

Circle the correct answer:

Class D. Class C. Class B.

↓↓**ANSWER**↓↓

Class B. (AIM 3-5-6 TRSA.)

Explanation: Both Class B structures and TRSA structures have multiple layers of airspace, with a constant ceiling across all layers and floors of varying height. Both Class B and TRSA may be thought of as an "upside down wedding cake" in structure. Class C airspace generally has only 2 layers of airspace. Class D airspace generally has only 1 layer of airspace.

2. In a TRSA, ATC controls aircraft in a manner that most closely resembles which other class of airspace?

Circle the correct answer:

Class D.   Class C.   Class B.

↓↓ANSWER↓↓

Class C. (AIM 3-5-6 c. TRSA.)

Explanation: An approach controller working TRSA airspace will assign your aircraft headings to help sequence you for landing at an airport within the TRSA. Approach will also provide traffic separation for IFR. Advisories and safety alerts are also available.

3. A TRSA has zero federal regulations that address operations specific to the TRSA airspace.

Circle the correct answer:

True.   False.

↓↓ANSWER↓↓

True.

Explanation: Hard to believe, but true!

4. When entering a TRSA, you are required to make radio contact with the approach control facility providing radar service within the TRSA.

Circle the correct answer:

Yes.   No.   Maybe.

↓↓ANSWER↓↓

No. (AIM 3-5-6 c. TRSA.)

5. While operating in a TRSA, are you required to participate in any aspect of radar service offered in the TRSA?

Circle the correct answer:

Yes. No. Maybe.

↓↓ANSWER↓↓

No. (AIM 3-5-6 c. TRSA.)

6. If you don't participate in radar service within a TRSA, you must contact the tower controller before penetrating the Class D airspace within a TRSA.

Circle the correct answer:

True. False.

↓↓ANSWER↓↓

True.

Explanation: Class D operations are not affected by the TRSA in any way. You must always establish contact with an airport tower inside Class D before entering Class D airspace.

For a complete discussion of TRSAs, see *Radio Mastery for VFR Pilots*, p. 301.

Think Like a Controller

You are working as an approach controller at O'Hare International Airport, Chicago. It is 1700 local time, and your Class B airspace is jam-packed with airliners landing and departing at O'Hare. You receive a radio call from Piper 9274L requesting a transition through the southwest corner of your sector. You have no time to work with this aircraft.

1. What do you transmit in reply to the VFR pilot requesting the transition?

↓↓**ANSWER**↓↓

"Piper 9274L, O'Hare Approach, unable your request. Remain clear of the Class Bravo."

2. You are working as an approach controller at the facility serving the Class B airspace surrounding Phoenix Sky Harbor Airport. A pilot checks on your frequency and tells you he is holding at 4,500 (below the floor of the Class B) over South Mountain. He tells you he would like to fly northbound on the published VFR transition corridor through your airspace. You check your radar screen and see a VFR radar target at 4,500 feet over South Mountain. After telling this pilot to remain clear of the Class Bravo, what will you tell the pilot to do before you clear him to make the transition? (Hint: It has something to do with the VFR target on your radar screen.)

↓↓**ANSWER**↓↓

You tell him to squawk a specific transponder code to identify his aircraft.

3. It is 0130 local time at the Hartsfield-Jackson International Airport. You are working as an approach and departure controller for the Class Bravo airspace over the airport. There is no IFR traffic in your airspace, so you approved a VFR pilot to transition through the Class Bravo. You assigned this pilot an altitude of 4,000 for the passage through your airspace. He reaches the outer boundary of the Class Bravo. You tell him, "Radar service terminated, squawk 1200," and what else?

↓↓**ANSWER**↓↓

"Resume VFR altitudes and frequency change approved."

4. You are working the approach control position for the TRSA over Montgomery, Alabama. You have several VFR aircraft in your airspace, including Super Cub 405UW. It appears another VFR aircraft might

cross paths with the Super Cub. You are not tasked with providing minimum separation between VFR aircraft in your airspace, but you are also responsible for making sure aircraft do not collide. What can you say to the pilot of the Super Cub if he tells you he does not see the traffic in conflict with his flight path?

↓↓ANSWER↓↓

"Super Cub 405UW, would you like a vector to avoid the traffic?" Or, you can skip the question and suggest a heading to avoid the traffic.

Most Important Takeaways

We have covered all of the scenarios you are most likely to encounter when working with ATC while VFR. I hope you detected important recurring ideas as you worked your way through the exercises. In this section, we will recap the most important takeaways from this training.

1. Which action gives you the greater advantage when operating in areas with a high density of air traffic?

Place a check mark next to the correct answer:

      1. _____ Visually scanning for traffic from the cockpit.

      2. _____ Visually scanning for traffic from the cockpit and receiving traffic alerts from ATC.

↓↓ANSWER↓↓

      2. Visually scanning for traffic from the cockpit and receiving traffic alerts from ATC.

2. Which action gives you the greater advantage when operating in areas of high terrain or tall obstructions?

Place a check mark next to the correct answer:

      1. _____ Visually scanning for terrain and obstructions from the cockpit.

      2. _____ Visually scanning for terrain and obstructions from the cockpit and receiving terrain/obstruction alerts from ATC.

↓↓ANSWER↓↓

      2. Visually scanning for terrain and obstructions from the cockpit and receiving terrain/obstruction alerts from ATC.

3. Which requires the lowest cockpit workload when your weather becomes marginal VFR?

Place a check mark next to the correct answer:

1. _____ Contacting ATC or FSS for weather information updates.

2. _____ Tuning in various AWOS/ASOS/ATIS stations to determine where the best weather conditions are located.

↓↓ANSWER↓↓

1. Contacting ATC or FSS for weather information updates.

4. If you are a student pilot, are you allowed to alert ATC that you are a student pilot in your initial radio call to the controller?

Circle the correct answer:

Yes.   No.

↓↓ANSWER↓↓

Yes.

Explanation: Not only are you allowed to tell ATC you are a student pilot, you *should* tell ATC you are a student pilot, to get the best handling for your level of experience.

5. If you tell the controller you are a student pilot upon initial contact, how will the controller change the delivery of his clearances when speaking to you?

_____

_____

↓↓ANSWER↓↓

The controller will slow his delivery; keep his instructions short; and allow more time for you to respond.

6. Even though it is not required of controllers, will a controller adjust the rate and complexity of his clearances if he detects your radio calls are not consistent with a highly experienced pilot?

Circle the most probable answer:

Probably.   Probably not.

↓↓**ANSWER**↓↓

Probably.

Explanation: Adjusting to a pilot's level of experience is part of an air traffic controller's training. Not all controllers will adjust to accommodate you. Some may not slow down if they are very busy. Some may continue to talk quickly out of habit. Most will do their best to help you out.

8. Knowing what you now know about air traffic control, would you say controllers deliver clearances:

Circle the correct answer:

In fairly consistent patterns.   In random, unpredictable fashion.

↓↓**ANSWER**↓↓

In fairly consistent patterns.

9. Why is using standard phraseology on the aircraft radio so important?

_____

_____

_____

_____

↓↓**ANSWER**↓↓

Any answer that gets these points across is correct: Using standard phraseology prevents confusion on the radio. When all air traffic controllers and all pilots make radio transmissions using standard phraseology, everyone on the radio frequency should be able understand what is happening, no matter where they operate.

10. If you clearly heard an ATC clearance, but did not understand what is expected of you, what should you do?

_____

↓↓**ANSWER** ↓↓

Ask the controller for clarification.

11. Let's say you ask ATC for clarification about a clearance, but you still don't understand what ATC said, even after the second attempt. What should you do now?

_____

_____

↓↓**ANSWER** ↓↓

Ask the controller to rephrase the clearance.

12. If a controller speaks at a rate that is too fast for you to understand, what should you say to the controller?

_____

_____

↓↓**ANSWER** ↓↓

"Please say again slower."

13. You are in contact with an enroute air traffic control center for VFR flight following. Other than having to acknowledge an occasional radio call, are you more restricted in where you can fly or in what you can do in your airplane than if you were not in contact with ATC?

Circle the correct answer:

Yes. No. Maybe.

↓↓ANSWER↓↓

No.

Explanation: Yes, I know there are some pilots who feel restricted by having to report altitude changes and by having to respond to traffic callouts. (Oh, it's just so much work!) For all practical purposes, you may still fly where you want to fly, and do what you want to do even when using flight following services.

14. In which situation are you likely to get the most rapid access to help when an emergency develops?

Place a check mark next to the correct answer:

1. _____ When you are already in contact with ATC.

2. _____ When you are not currently in contact with ATC.

↓↓ANSWER↓↓

1. When you are already in contact with ATC.

15. When operating in areas where Basic Radar Service for VFR Aircraft is offered (outside of Class B airspace), are you required to participate in radar service?
Circle the correct answer:

Yes. No. Maybe.

↓↓ANSWER↓↓

No.

16. What are some of the advantages of participating in Basic Radar Service for VFR Aircraft in terminal areas?

_____

_____

_____

_____

↓↓**ANSWER** ↓↓

You get radar sequencing with other aircraft inbound and outbound from the airport using radar service. Traffic advisories and traffic alerts are provided as well. Altitude alerts may also be provided.

17. Given all you now know about ATC, including the advantages, and what some might call disadvantages, are you now more likely to:

Note: No one will see or rate your answer. The choice you make is entirely yours, so please answer honestly. If it will produce the most honest answer, don't even check your choice below. Simply make a mental note of the answer that most applies to you.

_____ Contact ATC when and where ATC service is offered.

_____ Contact ATC only when absolutely required.

_____ Avoid contact with ATC as much as possible.

Stay True to the Standards and You Will Be Fine

I truly hope you enjoyed this workbook. I also hope it helped you improve the mental processes that apply to your radio work. The key to making these processes last is to practice them as often as possible. The only way to practice is to get out there and make some radio calls.

As you practice, please stay true to standard phraseology. Trust me, you are going to hear other pilots make radio transmissions that have nothing to do with the standards. Most of the time, ATC is going to let pilots say non-standard words without correcting them. That does not mean non-standard phraseology is okay. It only means air traffic controllers are not required to be teachers and disciplinarians.

Set a Goal

When practicing your radio work, you have to be your own teacher and evaluator. Set a goal to always use standard phraseology and stick to it, no matter what you hear others doing. Time and again, pilots have proven that using standard phraseology is safest. Using slang and other non-standard words is not only discouraged in various manuals, the use of non-standard phraseology has proven to be part of the causal chain in many deadly aircraft accidents.

Even if a pilot who uses non-standard phraseology flies for a lifetime without bending metal on his airplane, sooner or later, saying the wrong thing at the wrong time is going to get him in some form of trouble. Pilots have been known to fly off altitude, off route, or far too close to another airplane. The culprit is almost always misunderstanding on the radio.

Do a Small Favor for Others

How about doing a small favor for other pilots by giving feedback on the value of this workbook? Go to the listing for this workbook at Amazon.com and write a review in the comments section. Your opinion counts!

Stay in Touch

If you have questions now, or have questions in the future about aircraft radio communication, you may find the answers you are seeking in several places. My book *Radio Mastery for VFR Pilots* goes hand in hand with this workbook. My website, *http://ATCcommunication.com* has a wealth of information on aircraft radio work including in-depth articles and hours of free podcasts. I regularly update my Twitter feed: atc_jeff with tips about working with ATC. There are other great resources for practicing radio work, including a hands-on aircraft radio simulator at *http://ATCinsider.com. ATCinsider.com* is a free membership website for pilots.

If you cannot find what you are looking for at any of those sources, feel free to write to me at jeff@ATCcommunication.com. If I don't immediately have the answer you need, I sure know where to find it.

Until we talk to each other, on the radio or on the web . . .

Be well and fly safe,

Jeff

Made in the USA
Middletown, DE
22 October 2017